"The work of faith communities cannot be a solitary endeavor restricted to one particular population or age group. Meredith Gould helps readers understand the value of creating sacred space for one another to explore our purposes, identities, and legacies as a people of faith while drawing upon generational experiences. She explains how sociology and psychology intersect with Incarnational identities as people of faith. Anyone seeking deeper relationships and understanding within their communities needs to read—and use—this book. *Transcending Generations* helped me facilitate intergenerational groups who are looking to have honest conversations about growing faith and strengthening bonds."

—Rev. Tuhina Verma Rasche

"*Transcending Generations* helps us understand the ages and generations of adulthood in a new and refreshing way. At the heart of this book is the central insight that all adults—across all generations—share common core issues: identity, purpose, belonging, and legacy. Presenting these core issues from developmental and generational perspectives provides the understanding necessary for learning how to develop cross-generational conversations, relationships, and ministry. Practical ideas and strategies provide tools for fostering conversation and relationship building. Meredith Gould has written an essential and timely resource."

—John Roberto
  LifelongFaith Associates
  Co-author of *Seasons of Adult Faith Formation*
    and *Generations Together*

"*Transcending Generations* is a resource that is long overdue. This book is filled with helpful insights for organizations and faith communities seeking to understand and benefit from differences in generations. Meredith Gould offers a way for individuals and groups to maneuver successfully through the challenges and changes of life."

—Rev. Dr. Richard W Rouse, ELCA pastor and author of *Beyond Church Walls: Cultivating a Culture of Care* (Fortress Press)

"As a young pastor, I experienced the shifting and changing environment of generational church differences every day. Meredith Gould provides an indispensable guide for congregations to explore the nature of human development, shifting culture, dealing with differences, and change. *Transcending Generations* lays everything on the table for pastors, church leadership, staff, and laity to navigate ministry in the 21st century. I wish I had this book 10 years ago."

—Rev. Alan R. Rudnick, pastor and author of
The Work of The Associate Pastor (Judson Press)

"In a culture (and sometimes a church) that separates and stresses differences, Meredith Gould has given us a treasure that is so needed—thoughts and practices that accentuate our unity, our alikeness. Her book is filled with new insights, reflective questions, and perceptive exercises. You'll find yourself highlighting every other line! In addition to being a 'workbook' for collaboration, *Transcending Generations* would be a superb resource for an individual and/or group retreat. Gould provides all this in an easy-to-read, enjoyable style while challenging us to grow more deeply, relate more humanely, and serve more generously."

—Janet Schaeffler, OP
Author of *Deepening Faith: Adult Faith Formation
in the Parish* (Liturgical Press)

Transcending Generations

A Field Guide
to Collaboration in Church

Meredith Gould, PhD

LITURGICAL PRESS

Collegeville, Minnesota

www.litpress.org

1   2   3   4   5   6   7   8   9

Library of Congress Cataloging-in-Publication Data

Names: Gould, Meredith, 1951– author.
Title: Transcending generations : a field guide to collaboration in church / Meredith Gould, PhD.
Description: Collegeville, Minnesota : Liturgical Press, 2017. | Includes bibliographical references and index.
Identifiers: LCCN 2017029240 (print) | LCCN 2017005967 (ebook) | ISBN 9780814645871 (ebook) | ISBN 9780814645628
Subjects: LCSH: Intergenerational relations—Religious aspects—Christianity.
Classification: LCC BV640 (print) | LCC BV640 .G68 2017 (ebook) | DDC 253—dc23
LC record available at https://lccn.loc.gov/2017029240

*For those seeking what our generations share
and rejoicing in what is discovered.*

Contents

Preface

We had met on Twitter years earlier while participating in public conversations. Soon we were commiserating via private messages about the way things should be, especially in church. Now we were in my kitchen debating how social activism should play out, especially in church. He stabbed the air with horn fingers while making his next point, "Yo Meredith, dude, you're more Millennial than most Millennials I know."

I believe I was age sixty-three. I think he was age twenty-nine—or maybe thirty-one? Can't remember. Doesn't matter. We've always engaged as peers. We work together well and then super-collaboratively when our respective experiences and skill sets need a boost (or a jolt). Age has nothing to do with our mutual respect.

Not-all-that-strange and very true: during the past twenty years I've related best with people at least half my chronological age and at least one generation removed from my own cohort. I credit two life-changing events for my attitudes and outlook. In 1994, I got my body, mind, and spirit into twelve-step recovery. In 2008, I got onto—and very much into—social media.

Twelve Step recovery programs have always been excellent examples of intergenerational community, especially as increasingly younger young adults decide to clean up and sober up. Social media makes it possible to interact without knowing anyone's age, ethnicity, gender, race, religion, or other identifiers that typically get in the way. My ongoing experience is that by the time I choose to disclose my chronological age, mutually enriching friendships are so well established that peeps usually respond with a grittier version of "No way!"

Sad-but-true: I've *never* experienced this level of engagement among adults in church-the-building or any other community that relies on face-to-face interaction to build and sustain itself.

Wondering what else might be going on, I had a bunch of online conversations. I used social media best practices to either ask questions or make observations about age-based assumptions during other people's conversations. In December 2015, I moderated one of The Slate Project's weekly Twitter-based chats, asking a series of questions within this framework: What might become possible for the world of church if we remove age barriers to communication and collaboration?[1]

I discovered what I already know is true sociologically: (1) there are always more differences *within* groups than between them; (2) chronological age neither explains nor predicts much of anything; and (3) well-meaning people tend to confuse and collapse chronological age, psychosocial development, and generational cohort. And so I did what I usually do, I decided to write a book to explain why this happens and suggest another way to approach collaboration in church.

Transcending Generations is a guide to reviewing and rethinking the age-based assumptions undermining collaboration among adults. Each section opens with a brief synopsis of its chapters, but here's an overview of the entire book:

Section I: Frameworks for Understanding provides a critical look at why age-based assumptions emerged and how they're perpetuated. I describe if, when, and how chronological age, psychosocial (lifecycle) development, and generational cohort distinctions might be at all useful for understanding the attitudes and behaviors of adult congregants. This first section ends with a short chapter about stereotyping in general and ageism in particular.

Section II: In Every Generation focuses on concerns shared by adults across generations. I've identified these core issues: identity (Who am I?), purpose (Why am I here?), belonging (Where do I belong?), and legacy (How will I be remembered?). I explain why these concerns transcend generation, provide self-directed exercises for "Exploring the Challenges," and suggest ways to have collaborative conversations.

Section III: Moving Forward Together has chapters about cultivating these core skills: listening, decision-making, and embracing change. You'll find practical tips in two appendices: Listening 101 and Decision-Making 101.

As is the case with all of my books, I include questions for individual inquiry and group discussion with every chapter. Just so you know, I ask myself these questions to monitor my own attitudes and assumptions about others. Always and forever working on that particular human frailty, so help me God.

An important note about terms. You may notice that while I use the terms "cross-generational" and "intergenerational" interchangeably, I typically specify "adults of all ages." I do this to highlight my intentional focus on—wait for it—adults of all ages! At the same time, I reference valuable contributions of intergenerational/cross-generational faith formation experts who focus on bringing together children, teens, young adults, middle-aged adults, and older adults for education, service, and worship. I've written *Transcending Generations* to be used in tandem with their work, especially by congregations that view young adults (ages 18–30) as being more similar to teens than older adults. You'll find more about age categorization and nomenclature in section I.

Two additional comments about reading. First, please read the chapters in sequence. Depending on your level of expertise and experience, you might feel tempted to skip chapters in section I. Please at least skim them. Second, I invite you to read the endnotes. If you're familiar with my work, you already know why I'm extending this invitation. If you're a first-time reader, you'll discover commentary, ruminations, and self-disclosures along with citations and resources (with online links).

As ever, hopes inspired me to write *Transcending Generations*. Hopes kept me going when I wanted to quit writing it. First and foremost, I hope that we come to understand, at a core level, that what unites our generations is more significant than anything dividing us. And I hope that we embrace this understanding to serve God and one another here and now.

Acknowledgments

I'm hyperbolically super-deeply grateful for the generous, smart, and wise support I receive at every stage of a book project. Conversations with Rev. Evan Dolive, Rev. David Hansen, Rev. Kyle Oliver, and Rev. Sarah Napoline were an important part of this book's development. Their observations and questions helped me move from maybe possibly writing something about cross-generational ministry to the book proposal stage.

During the writing stage of this book, my work was enhanced by valuable critique (vs. criticism, see p. 87) from first readers—John Deuel, whose line edits were perfect; Ruth Harrigan, who is my forever first among first readers; and Regina Heater, whose questions helped me avoid conceptual bloopers. Hosanna-like shout-out to Rev. Jason Chesnut for reviewing and suggesting Bible verses and to Deacon Tara Ulrich, who responded in real time to a frantic Twitter inquiry about Scripture.

Notable among those providing comfort, especially via the back channel: @JesusofNaz316, Rev. Aaron Billard, Rev. Laurie Brock, Rev. Lisa Holliday, Rev. Kathi Johnson, Rev. Carol Howard Merritt, Rev. Alan Rudnick, and Fran Rossi Szpylczyn. This is also the second book during which I sought coaching from Rev. Laurie J. Ferguson, PhD, and after which I announced how I was loath to write another book without her. Ever.

Living with a writer is not for the faint of heart or weak in spirit. Fortunately, my spouse Rev. Canon Dan Webster has a generous heart and strong spirit, plus the wisdom to recognize and forgive book-writing-induced insanity. Thanks hon!

Transcending Generations is the third book that I've been privileged to publish with Liturgical Press. I was happy and relieved when this band got back together: Andy Edwards in editorial; Michelle Verkuilen in marketing; Colleen Stiller, Stephanie Nix, and Julie Surma in production; and Barry Hudock managing the team. And yet another great cover design by and creative process with Stefan Killen.

Always and forever, thanks be to God.

SECTION I
Frameworks for Understanding

Assumptions about chronological age, psychosocial development, and generational cohort can get in the way of successful collaboration among adults. In this section, I provide a crash refresher course in the basics and beyond.

CHAPTER 1
About Age and Aging

— Someone will always be—or seem—older or younger than you, and you'll probably have opinions about them based on assumptions about their chronological age. Your parents? You may think they're ridiculously old and know next to nothing. Ironically, your grandparents probably think your parents are ridiculously young and don't know enough. Perhaps you think your pastor is too young (or too old) and really should know better.

Recently, after doing some simple arithmetic I realized that my high school teachers who then seemed so old were probably much younger than I am right now. And depending on the day, I don't consider myself old, although I'm probably older than you—chronologically.

Age is commonly defined as the length of time someone has lived. That's it! A number of chronological years for corporeal existence. Still, this straightforward definition doesn't seem to stop many of us from adding layers of meaning to the word "age" as well as to specific numbers. Distorted meaning.

What thoughts spring immediately to mind when you read "age 23"? How about when you read "age 68"? Notice the subtle or not-so-subtle shift in your 'tude when age 68 is rounded up to age 70. Many of your automatic assumptions about age will impede successful collaboration with adults across generations.

3

Am I suggesting that we completely ignore chronological age and aging? Not at all. I'd simply like us to learn more about if and when chronological age might be a useful variable.

Chronological age is a useful variable for understanding two things: (1) human brain development and (2) longevity—that is, how long someone is likely to live. Beyond that? Not much. Even psychologists who agree about the significance of chronological age for cognitive, emotional, and behavioral development in children do not agree about its explanatory value for adult development (see chapter 2: Exploring Psychosocial Development).

First, let's focus on the human brain. The human brain is a three-pound organ with a complex network of a bazillion cells. Knowing how it develops should help you rethink expectations about what you believe young adults (i.e., adults ages 18–35) should be capable of doing. (Spoiler Alert: Many of your expectations are unreasonable and unfair.)

We have modern neuroscience to thank for revealing that the human brain develops well into young adulthood. The prefrontal cortex is still under construction even when the rest of the body may have (or seems to be) physically matured. It turns out that the brain doesn't reach full maturity until around age 25—and possibly as late as the early thirties. This is important information. Until our prefrontal cortex fully develops, our ability to pay attention, control impulses, think logically, engage in complex planning, and make decisions will be underdeveloped.[1]

Let that sink in, especially if this evidenced-based information comes as news. Take a deep breath. Exhale. Note that laws establishing age of consent and criminal responsibility as well as driving, drinking, and voting age were passed long before we knew this much about brain development.

"Don't trust anybody over thirty."

An entire generation glommed onto and repeated "Don't trust anybody over thirty" like it was part of a catechism. The generation? Baby Boomers. The person who said it? Jack Weinberg, a student activist in the Berkeley Free Speech Movement. He was age 24 at the time. When was that? 1964. Are you now laugh-snorting, rolling your eyes, or quietly weeping?

Next, let's revisit what we currently know about life expectancy (i.e., longevity). Knowing how long anyone is likely to live should help you rethink expectations about the capabilities of older adults (i.e., adults age 65+). (Spoiler Alert: Many of your expectations are unreasonable and unfair.)

Demographers, who focus on sociological and economic variables, and gerontologists, who focus on biomedical factors, agree that race, ethnicity, sex (i.e., biological status as female or male), gender (i.e., identification as feminine, masculine, or neither), and socioeconomic status help predict longevity. They also agree that medical technology and increased public health awareness about disease prevention has significantly extended human life.[2] Researchers and clinicians in both fields view aging as a complex process. Aging involves physiological changes and progressive functional decline plus increased vulnerability to illness and disease. All of this happens within a socioeconomic context.

Context is important for understanding if and when chronological age is a significant factor for explaining just about anything. Take a look at data from the National Institute of Aging to see just how many problems of age-related decline have practically nothing to do with chronological age. Cognitive difficulties, for example, typically have more to do with addiction, boredom, depression, medications, and stress. Declining hand strength among men younger than age thirty has more to do with shifts from manual to technology-driven labor rather than chronological age.[3] Chronic illness and physical disability can occur at any age.

Point of Clarification: Gerontology and Geriatrics

Gerontology and geriatrics are professional disciplines that focus on aging and serve people in late adulthood (age 65+).

Gerontology: Multidisciplinary field focusing on the scientific study of aging. Gerontologists are trained primarily in social science but also in physiology plus public health and policy. Undergraduate and graduate programs in gerontology emerged after the Older American's Act (OAA) passed in 1965 and the Administration on Aging (AoA) provided funding to develop them.

Geriatrics: Medical specialty within adult internal medicine. Geriatricians provide medical support for normal healthy aging and also treat age-related diseases/conditions. Geriatrics was developed at the turn of the twentieth century by Dr. Ignatz Nascher, who first suggested the term in 1909 and published *Geriatrics: The Diseases of Old Age and Their Treatment* in 1914.

Gerontologists have taken on the heroic no-win task of creating subgroups to clarify who might be classified as "old" without enraging Baby Boomers (see chapter 3: Understanding Generations).

When the Social Security Administration (née Social Security Board) was established in 1935, it was okay to characterize people in their sixties as "the aged" or "elderly."[4] Within forty years those terms had become socially and politically intolerable (see chapter 4: A Bit about Stereotypes and Ageism). Need to test this? Tell your sixty-two-year-old choir director that she's elderly and get back to me about how that went.

Increased life expectancy combined with social awareness and activism led to crafting more socially acceptable terms for old age. And not just once but multiple times since the 1970s.

First, the words "older person" replaced the term "elderly." Next, gerontologists had to reconfigure age groupings because any variation on the word "old" had become overly broad and deeply offensive to at least some people.

These subgroups—Young-Old, Middle-Old, and Oldest-Old/Very Old—emerged without consensus about which age ranges to include. Did Young-Old span ages 60 to 69 or ages 65 to 74? Did Middle-Old age end at age 79 or age 84? Should octogenarians be called the Very Old, Oldest-Old, or Old-Old?[5] In some instances these categories were also used within geriatric medicine and for stages of psychosocial development—but not always.

In addition to solving (for now) problems of language and negative stereotyping, these categorizations may also have made it easier for medical practitioners to negotiate medical codes and reimbursement in the twenty-first century. But, really and truly, notice how swiftly the terminology for chronological age plunges you into a dense pile of assumptions about people in those subgroups. This is one ongoing challenge of collaboration among adults of all ages everywhere, not only within the world of church.

While knowing someone's birth year provides a valuable historical context and helps us define generational cohort, it can swiftly morph into something neither good nor helpful.[6] Go ahead and put it to this personal test: You find out someone's chronological age—and then what happens?

Want to collaborate with other adults? If so, you'll need to become super-conscious about what you think, believe, and might do as a result of knowing their chronological age. For the love of all that's holy, please don't be that person who, upon discovering someone's age, makes false assumptions about their emotional maturity or ability to collaborate.

Physical Condition	Related to Aging	May Occur At Any Age
Age-Related Dementia[7]	✓	
Cataracts	✓	
Collagen Loss	✓	
Gum Recession		✓
Hair Loss		✓
Hearing Loss		✓
Liver Spots	✓	
Loss of Balance		✓
Loss of Mobility		✓
Osteoarthritis	✓	
Reduced Bone Density		✓
Rheumatoid Arthritis		✓
Wrinkles	✓	

Your Reality Check-Up: About Age and Aging

Contemplate your current reality and move forward by discussing:

- What are my hopes and fears about aging?

- What do I need to de-romanticize about being younger?

- How might my attitudes about becoming or being old be influencing my church participation?

CHAPTER 2
Exploring Psychosocial Development

Act your age! How old are you? And my personal favorite: What are you, twelve?

What seem like references to chronological age are, more accurately, snarky digs about emotional development or lack thereof. Emotional development is, in part, what psychologists mean by psychosocial or lifecycle development. The "in part" part reflects how theories have changed since the late nineteenth and early twentieth centuries. Back then, psychologists believed that personality and other manifestations of identity were firmly established during childhood and tied to age-related growth.

By the 1950s, however, traditional (read: Freudian) theories of personality development based on physiological things like breast feeding and potty training had been revised to recognize the impact of social institutions and interactions. These days you'll have difficulty finding a psychologist (or psychotherapist) still clinging to the belief that biology is destiny. Ever-emerging information about the human genome makes that assertion obsolete. Nor do we have to delve too far back into psychology's intellectual history to find additional revisions to understanding human psychosocial development (a.k.a. the lifecycle).

First, the number of developmental stages have changed. How many there are depends on whose work you study and whether that theorist viewed emotional development as continuing during adulthood. You can find developmental theories with as few as four stages (Jung) and as many as twelve (Armstrong).[1]

I believe it's safe to say that most popular typologies linking biological and psychosocial development net out at eight stages because of Erik Erikson, who was influenced by Freud's main challenger, Carl Jung.

Development according to Carl Jung

Carl Jung (1875–1961) is typically credited for being the first to depart from Sigmund Freud's (1856–1939) biologically based psychosexual focus. Jung theorized that human development happens when opposing tensions (i.e., realizations) are reconciled during four sequential phases. Note: chronological ages in brackets are what Jung used for his typology developed during the 1930s.

Jung's Stages of Development

Stage I: Childhood (birth to adolescence)
Sporadic consciousness gives way to abstract and logical thinking
Outcome: ego development

Stage II: Youth & Early Years (adolescence to ages 35–40)
Growing consciousness and the realization that childhood is over
Outcome: independence, finding a mate, child rearing, and family life

Stage III: Middle Life (ages 40–60)
Realizations about mortality and questions about life's meaning
Outcome: turning inward, developing spiritual life

Stage IV: Old Age (age 60+)
Wise acceptance of life's realities
Outcome: reconciliation with inevitable death, hope for legacy

A number of factors inspired detailed typologies of psychosocial development. Enhanced knowledge about the human brain, for example, led to creating categories like School Age, Early Adolescence (Pre-Puberty), Adolescence, and Young Adulthood.[2] Increased longevity gave rise to identifying developmental tasks during what gerontologist Ken Dychtwald termed the "Third Age," sociologist Sara Lawrence-Lightfoot called "The Third Chapter," and the process characterized as "Sage-ing" by Rabbi Zalman Schacter-Shalomi.[3]

Development according to Erik Erikson

According to twentieth-century psychoanalyst Erik Erikson (1902–94), individuals develop by moving through eight sequential stages. Erikson identified nurture (socialization) as having as much impact as, if not more than, nature (biology).

Jung's impact on Erik Erikson becomes especially obvious when their developmental stages are studied in tandem. Note: chronological ages in brackets are what Erikson used for his typology developed during the 1950s.[4]

Erikson's Stages of Development

Stage I: Infancy (birth–18 months)
Resolving issues of basic trust vs. mistrust
Outcome: hope (i.e., optimism) and confidence

Stage II: Early Childhood/Toddler (18 months–3 years)
Struggling with autonomy vs. shame and doubt
Outcome: will (i.e., sense of pride) and independence

Stage III: Play Age/Preschooler (ages 3–5)
Exploring initiative vs. guilt
Outcome: courage, purpose, and curiosity

Stage IV: School Age (ages 6–12)
Wrestling with issues of industry vs. inferiority
Outcome: competence and self-esteem

Stage V: Adolescence (ages 12–18)
Managing identity vs. identity confusion
Outcome: fidelity to ideals, causes, and friends

Stage VI: Young Adulthood (ages 18–35)
Resolving intimacy vs. isolation
Outcome: love, deeper intimacy, and appreciating solitude

Stage VII: Adulthood (ages 35–55 or –65)
Resolving generativity (i.e., guiding the next generation)
vs. stagnation
Outcome: care and seeking to contribute something meaningful

Stage VIII: Late Adult/Old Age (ages 55– or 65–death)
Confronting integrity vs. despair and disgust
Outcome: wisdom and fulfillment

Currently in debate is a proposition that the transition between adolescence and adulthood is blurry enough to warrant a distinct category. Whether this new category called "Emerging Adulthood" and the corresponding process dubbed "adulting" has staying power remains to be seen.[5]

Articulating how (vs. when) individuals develop throughout the lifecycle has also changed. Theorists initially viewed development as sequential. Individuals moved from infancy through childhood to adolescence and adulthood in stages. Movement from one stage to the next depended on working through significant emotional tasks (a.k.a. crises, tensions, challenges).[6]

Academic psychologists and practicing psychotherapists also identified "arrested development" relative to mental and emotional growth. They've explained how psychosocial development can slow down significantly or screech to a halt for any number of reasons. The short list includes: death of or separation from a primary caregiver; substance abuse and addiction (by the individual or primary caregiver); physical abuse, trauma, and neglect; and acute or chronic physical illness.

By the late twentieth century, psychologists began focusing on the ongoing development of adults. Psychiatrist Roger Gould mapped a process of adulthood independent of parents. Assumptions about the timing, sequence, and hierarchy of emotional development were also challenged by psychologist Daniel Levinson.[7] Levinson invited researchers, observers, and therapists to think about sequential but *not* hierarchical transitions through eras of structure-building (e.g., starting a family) and structure-changing (e.g., change after major life events). Transitions from one era to the next, he argued, are as significant as the eras themselves.

Adult Development according to Daniel J. Levinson

Psychologist Daniel J. Levinson (1920–94) characterized the adult lifecycle as a series of overlapping eras. His assertions about family life and careers during Early Adult Transition and Early Adulthood may seem out of whack with current reality, but knowing about Levinson's theories is important. Note: chronological ages in brackets are what Levinson used for his typology developed during the late 1970s and 1980s.[8]

Levinson's Eras of Adult Development

Era I: Pre-adulthood (conception to about age 22)
> Growing from total dependency to the beginning of independent, responsible adulthood. Rapid physical growth.
> *Early Adult Transition* (about ages 17–22) provides a starting point for tasks during early adulthood. Physical growth complete. Independence established.

Era II: Early Adulthood (about ages 17–45)
> Time of great energy and abundance as well as contradiction and stress. Family life begins; shift from occupation to career.
> *Midlife Transition* (about ages 40–45) involves sudden and major changes. Questioning previous life choices.

Era III: Middle Adulthood (about ages 40–65)
> Dealing with changes in family relationship, physical health, impending retirement from work.
> *Late Adult Transition* (about ages 60–65) includes changes in health. Peers start dying. Facing fears of becoming old, boring, and irrelevant.

Era IV: Late Adulthood (about ages 60–85)
> Relinquishing formal power and authority, especially at work. Cultivating inner resources and unselfish interests. Balancing personal reflection with mentoring others.

In turn, all that theoretical work gave rise to another important shift in focus: social markers became viewed as significant indicators of adulthood. True adults, it was supposed, complete higher education, live independently, get married, start a family, and build a career—in that sequence. Keep reading before you hurl this book (or your Kindle) across the room.

Critics with either awareness of or training in social history soon pointed out how this so-called normal trajectory toward adulthood wasn't at all normative. Instead, it was an anomaly of the 1950s and 1960s.[9] You don't need to be an academically trained social scientist to recognize how the impact of economic factors (e.g., student loan debt, changes in the job and housing markets), political variables (e.g., wars and civil unrest), and sociocultural changes (e.g., increased acceptance of premarital cohabitation and childbearing) would render the sequence questionable if not irrelevant by now.

As ever, there are more and different ways to explore human development. Theorists have used age to define stages of faith and moral judgment, which I won't be detailing in this book.[10] I will, however, zoom in on Abraham Maslow's hierarchy of needs (see chapter 6: Purpose).

So how do psychosocial development theories help us identify barriers to collaboration? Well, like chronological age, the human lifecycle is an element to invoke with awareness and caution. The limitations of relying on psychosocial development theories have been underscored by experts who focus on Christian faith formation among children, adolescents, and adults.[11] I believe these limitations are equally true when identifying barriers to collaboration among adults.

Consider how collaboration among younger and older adults is enhanced by acknowledging that "coming-of-age" can happen at any stage of life. We're invited to believe that we can be "changed in a moment, in the twinkling of an eye" (1 Cor 15:52).

Then surely we might also believe that hearts, minds, and behaviors could be changed throughout adulthood.

 Your Reality Check-Up:
Exploring Psychosocial Development

Contemplate your current reality and move forward by discussing:

- What assumptions do I make about adult development?

- Which psychosocial theories about lifecycle development are most in alignment with my experience of adulthood?

- How have situations and experiences affected my adult development?

CHAPTER 3
Understanding Generations

No matter what your chronological age these scenarios are predictable and possibly inevitable:

Scenario 1: At a gathering with people from your generation, you catch yourself thinking, *"Oh dear God, I have nothing in common with these people."*

Scenario 2: At a gathering with people from a younger generation, you realize, *"Oh dear God, these people think I have nothing in common with them."*

Maybe this doesn't happen at a gathering but while you're stuck in a supermarket checkout line. Or maybe you have this revelation while sitting in a movie theater or attending a church picnic. *Your* church's picnic. Lord, have mercy.

At this point in the twenty-first century four generations share the world of work and at least four generations share the world of church.[1] Another one or two generations are likely to emerge during your lifetime, so for the sake of collaboration, we need to learn more about them. For that we turn to social scientists and others who have already researched, studied, and defined generational cohorts.[2]

Generational cohorts are defined by birth year and, until recently, in fifteen- to twenty-year chunks of time.[3] During the 1990s, Gail Sheehy made a strong case for slicing cohorts into shorter time periods, which was truly prophetic given how digital technology would speed up rates of sociocultural change during the twenty-first century.

Using birth year as a marker has a couple of key benefits. First, birth year makes it easier to pinpoint when a generation's members are adults according to chronological age. Focusing on birth year also makes it easier to recognize the significant historical events and cultural developments shaping each generation's attitudes, beliefs, values, and behaviors.

Generational Cohorts	
Name of Cohort	**Birth Years**[4]
Silent Generation	1928–45
Baby Boomers	1946–64
Generation X	1965–80
Millennials	1981–97
Generation Z	1998–TBD

To date, these generations have been clearly identified, defined, and named: Silent Generation, Baby Boomers, and Generation X.[5] Since the 1990s, researchers have had more difficulty choosing social, political, or economic markers to delineate GenXers from Millennials or GenZers. You'll also find somewhat less agreement about how to define Millennials and Generation Z because they've emerged within the previous decade or two.

Whether you review social science research or marketing manifestos, you'll find these commonly accepted distinctions:

- *Silent Generation:* practical, dedicated, patient, willing to delay gratification, and value loyalty. *Defining moments:* Great Depression, Pearl Harbor, Roosevelt's New Deal. *Parents of:* Baby Boomers.

- *Baby Boomers:* optimistic, driven, competitive, involved, committed to personal growth, and value social and political change. *Defining moments:* Civil Rights movement, Space Race, Vietnam War, Woodstock. Note: Baby Boomers became the largest living population in the United States in 2017. *Parents of:* GenXers and sometimes Millennials.

- *Generation X:* skeptical, outcome-focused, committed to diversity, self-reliant, globally aware, and value work-life balance. *Defining moments: Roe v. Wade*, AIDS, *Challenger* explosion, digital technology developments, Persian Gulf war, Oklahoma City bombing. *Parents of:* GenZers.

- *Millennials:* optimistic, ambitious, confident, impatient, involved, civic-minded, committed to diversity, and value inclusivity. *Defining moments:* Iraq and Afghanistan wars, September 11, Columbine and Virginia Tech shootings, Obama election. *Parents of:* GenZers.

- *Generation Z:* entrepreneurial, self-directed, compassionate, determined, resourceful, loyal, and value transparency (i.e., truth-telling). *Defining moments:* TBD. Note: Gen Z is the most diverse and multicultural of any generation in the United States.[6]

How accurate are these categories and their characteristics? Pretty accurate, but don't let that stop you from being an outlier! Have fun with one or more online tests to discover whether the generation to which you belong is the generation with which you most identify. You might discover that you, like I, am a Perennial.[7]

A Generation by Any Other Name . . .

Kudos, I suppose, to those trying to make their mark by re-naming generations, but I recommend using terms most likely to be recognized by the greatest number of people.[8] The following info should help you to avoid getting lost in translation. Keeping score at home? Notice how GenXers and Millennials are basically tied for the most insulting monikers.

Greatest Generation: World War II Generation

Silent Generation: G.I. Generation, Veterans, Lucky Few, Builder Generation, Traditionalists

Baby Boomers: Vietnam Generation, Postwar Generation, Sixties Generation, Me Generation

Generation X: Echo Boomers, Baby Busters, Thirteeners, Endangered Generation, Lost Generation, Hip-Hop Generation, Latchkey Generation, Slacker Generation, Middle Child Generation

Millennials: Generation Y, Peter Pan Generation, Trophy Generation, Bridger Generation, Always-On Generation, Internet Generation, Echo Boomerang, Mosaics, Post-Gen, GenDIY

Generation Z: Digital Natives, iGeneration, Generation Next

But wait, there's more!

Birth year does not account for nuances *within* generations.[9] Demographic variables come into play. As always, race, ethnicity, sex (i.e., biological status as male or female), gender (i.e., identification as feminine, masculine, or neither), and socioeconomic status have meaning and impact. Prime example from The Duh Department: a black woman born in 1953 does not share the same historical and cultural experience as a white man born in 1953—or ever.[10] Add geography and socioeconomic status and watch more differences emerge, underscoring why studying generations is such a complex enterprise and yet another variable to invoke with extreme caution.[11]

Once again, I get edgy-cranky about anyone making assumptions, this time about how generations diverge in attitude and behavior. What you might consider a generation gap may not be as significant (and certainly not as unique) as you might expect—or hope.[12]

While one generation's music might be another generation's noise, Boomers, Millennials, and GenZers are passionate about social justice and spiritual awareness. Shared values make sense when you zoom in on who has done or is currently doing the parenting. Also keep in mind that your defining moments might not be anywhere near—let alone on the radar of—people in younger cohorts. Conversely, your defining moments might either be minimized or dismissed with a shrug by those in older cohorts.

Finally, some generations simply haven't been around long enough for anyone to collect anything more than anecdotes about attitudes and behaviors. Many speculations about the future attitudes and behaviors of GenZers are just that—speculations whose validity rests on the agenda of those doing the speculating.

Not-So-Great Expectations

Tensions between generations can be explained, in part, by not-so-great expectations. After conducting studies with thousands of students, psychologists Susan Fiske and Michael North identified three dominant stereotypes younger people have about what "old people should" (or should not) be doing:

Succession: Having already "had their turn," older people should get out of the way (i.e., "How can I advance my career if your generation still rules everything?")

Consumption: Since they're approaching end of life, older people should relinquish limited resources (i.e., "By the time I'm old, your generation will have trashed Medicare and Social Security.")

Identity: Older people should adhere to age-appropriate behavior (i.e., "Stop trying to hijack my awesomeness.")

Good news: This research has expanded conversations about age-based discrimination beyond descriptive stereotypes (i.e., how people are) to consider the impact of prescriptive stereotypes (i.e., how people should be).

Bad news: Their research identifies young people "as the greatest perpetrators of age-based 'shoulds,'" but remember these findings are based on responses from college undergraduates.[13]

Generations are often characterized too broadly and therefore inaccurately. You can avoid tumbling into and getting stuck in that trap by committing to things like conscious listening (see appendix A: Listening 101).

Knowing more about generational cohorts helps us distinguish between what may be due to historical timing and what, if anything (translation: precious little!), is due to chronological age or psychosocial development. I believe that using what we know about generations will make it easier to work together within and for church.[14] We want to reduce perceived gaps between generations, not make them wider and deeper. In the end, adults of all ages want the same things—to be valued and respected, to belong, to make a difference and leave a legacy.

Your Reality Check-Up:
Understanding Generations

Contemplate your current reality and move forward by discussing:

- Which moments in history have I experienced as defining? How would my parents answer? My grandparents?

- What about my generation do I want people from previous and subsequent generations to appreciate?

- How might I use information about generations to reduce intergenerational confusion and conflict?

CHAPTER 4

A Bit about Stereotypes and Ageism

Perhaps simply reading the word "stereotype" makes you cringe. It immediately conjures up the specter of mean-spirited, negative, and distorted (if not flat-out wrong) characterizations. And you, being a follower of Jesus, would *never* use them. Not consciously, anyway. Well, brace yourself for an encounter with social psychological reality.

While you may not be actively ascribing negative characteristics to entire groups of people, you do make generalizations about them. That's okay, we all do—some of us more often than others if it's our academic specialty.[1]

Generalizations are not inherently bad. Humans sort things—including other humans—into categories and then make generalizations. Social scientists view this as normative and are remarkably aligned about the cultural, social, and psychological value of making generalizations. For anthropologists, generalizations are useful for organizing and understanding cultural identity. For sociologists, generalizations function to create and sustain social order. Psychologists use generalizations to help individuals understand personality types and social identity.

Social Identity according to Henri Tajfel and John Turner

In 1979, British psychologists Henri Tajfel (1919–82) and John Turner (1947–2011) made an important contribution to social psychology. Their social identity theory explains how stereotyping clarifies identity and enhances self-image.[2]

Mental Processes of Creating Social Identity

First Mental Process: Social Categorization
  Categorizing people to identify and understand them.
  Result: Insight about ourselves.

Second Mental Process: Social Identification
  Discovering the group to which we belong and then adopting that group's identity.
  Result: Developing in-group identity (i.e., sense of "us").

Third Mental Process: Social Comparison
  Comparing our group with other groups. Favorable comparisons reinforce in-group belonging, while negative comparisons help define out-groups.
  Result: Self-esteem boosted and maintained by in-group identity.

Nor do generalizations automatically morph into stereotypes. Stereotypes are extreme generalizations that ignore diversity within groups, and there are typically more differences *within* groups than between them. For example, paying attention to differences in socioeconomic status should undermine stereotypes of entire racial-ethnic groups.[3] If stereotyping "all women" or "all men" ever made any sense, it no longer does so as we learn more about gender identity relative to physiological sex.[4] But because they're rooted in emotion, stereotypes not only endure but are perpetuated.

In addition, stereotypes can be negative or positive. Negative stereotypes lead to biased attitudes (i.e., prejudice) and behavior (i.e., discrimination) detrimental to individuals, specific groups, and society as a whole. Positive stereotypes usually remain unchallenged because they seem benign. But positive stereotypes can cause harm in their own dubiously positive way. Imagine, for example, what middle school must be like for Asian American kids who suck at math.[5]

Point of Clarification: Generalizations and Stereotypes

While every stereotype is a generalization, not all generalizations are stereotypes. Still, that doesn't stop people from using the terms interchangeably. Reduce stressful confusion by distinguishing generalizations from stereotypes and encouraging your dialogue partners to do likewise.

Generalizations are broad statements that:
- describe groups of people based on careful observation and experience;
- represent a rational effort to categorize;
- focus on accuracy;
- facilitate understanding; and
- change as new information becomes available.

Stereotypes are broad statements that:
- judge groups of people based on unexamined emotions and experience;
- represent an irrational effort to classify;
- focus on oversimplification;
- facilitate divisiveness; and
- remain fixed and impervious to new information.

Point of Clarification:
Prejudice and Discrimination

Yes of course there's a strong relationship between attitudes and behavior, but someone can be a "prejudiced non-discriminator" or a "non-prejudiced discriminator." Distinguishing prejudice from discrimination could reduce stress during difficult conversations.

Prejudice: Emotionally charged and negatively biased beliefs and value judgments about a social group, not necessarily anchored in personal experience. Prejudice, whether blatantly obvious or subtly cloaked, is an attitudinal extension of negative stereotypes. Reduced or eliminated by: revealing disconnects between beliefs and empirical realities; meaningful interaction with the so-called Other.

Discrimination: Unfair treatment based on biased thoughts, feelings, and attitudes about a social group. Discrimination, whether blatantly illegal or subtle stigmatization and exclusion, is a behavioral extension of negative stereotypes. Reduced or eliminated by: laws requiring equal treatment.

As for why stereotypes emerge and persist, here again social scientists are in alignment. Even when filtered through (allegedly) distinct theoretical lenses anthropologists, sociologists, and psychologists view stereotypes as social constructs for maintaining order, control, and power. Cultures seek to control dominant stories about values and beliefs (a.k.a, ethos). Dominant groups seek to retain power by controlling social stratification and stigmatizing outgroup members. Individuals struggle to establish and sustain identity as well as ways to belong.

Thinking, theorizing, talking, and writing about stereotypes and prejudice emerged during the 1920s, which makes this a relatively new intellectual enterprise. No surprise there because so are the social sciences, which began developing as academic disciplines around the same time. Before the social sciences were invented questions about human thought and behavior were discussed primarily in philosophy departments. Critical inquiry into the insidious and, for that matter, invidious consequences of prejudice and discrimination didn't emerge for another couple of decades.[6] Researchers, clinicians, public policy wonks, and social activists focused on race and ethnicity before paying any attention to sexism. The notion, let alone reality, that age might be subject to stereotyping, prejudice, and discrimination didn't make it into public awareness until the late 1960s. When it did, the emphasis was on attitudes and behaviors of "young people" toward "old people" as defined by chronological age.

Ageism

Prejudice and discrimination based on chronological age wasn't called "ageism" until 1969. Dr. Robert N. Butler, founding director of the National Institute of Aging, coined the term during an interview about housing discrimination in the *Washington Post*.

Later in *The Gerontologist*, he would prophetically observe that "age-ism [sic] might parallel (it might be wishful thinking to say replace) racism as the great issue of the next 20 to 30 years."

Butler's advocacy efforts focused on elderly adults when "elderly" was defined as age 65 and older. Today, the term "ageism" is also applied to age-based discrimination against young people, especially young adults.[7]

Here we are, half a century later, and almost everything about age and ageism tends to be a messy mashup of assumptions about chronological age and aging, psychosocial development, and generational cohort. Factoring in race, ethnicity, and gender adds complexity to our conversations about age.

The key question for us is: What difference do age differences make? We now have research revealing a correlation between ageist stereotypes of older people and negative health outcomes.[8] Ageism runs deep. Prejudice based on age-related status(es) seems to be tolerated in ways that prejudice about other groups is not, even by those who are swift to call out prejudice based on other features of identity.

Attitudes, assumptions, and beliefs about age are slow to change. So is behavior, despite laws to prevent age discrimination, as well as procedures for punishing those doing the discriminating. We don't have a prayer of getting far with collaboration among adults until we consciously and carefully unpack everything stuffed into this baggage. Come to think of it, prayer might be an excellent way of moving forward to heal disappointments, bridge divides, and explore beliefs about identity, purpose, belonging, and legacy shared by all adults.

| Just a Few Age-Related Stereotypes ||
Old(er) People	Young(er) People
Bad Drivers (too damn slow)	Bad Drivers (too damn fast)
Smelly and Sloppy	Sloppy and Smelly
No Filters (can say anything)	No Filters (will say anything)
Can't Remember Stuff	Won't Remember Stuff
Grumpy, Entitled, and Self-absorbed	Self-absorbed, Entitled, and Oppositional
Apathetic and Won't Collaborate	Apathetic and Can't Collaborate

Your Reality Check-Up:
Stereotypes and Ageism

Contemplate your current reality and move forward by discussing:

- Which stereotypes about age, lifecycle development, or generations do I secretly believe are probably true?

- When have I experienced discrimination based on my chronological age or generation?

- How has ageism affected my ability to collaborate with people older and younger than me?

SECTION II
In Every Generation

Core concerns about identity, purpose, belonging, and legacy unite adults of all ages. In this section, I offer a closer look at why and how to have collaborative conversations that transcend generations.

CHAPTER 5
Identity

Identity is more of a mind-bending shapeshifter than anyone ever expects it to be. The identity you considered primary at one point in your life will shift to something else over time and according to circumstances. Your identity as an employee will shift with promotions and again if you move into management. You'll be a parent in perpetuity, but that identity shifts as your children grow older, especially if they become responsible for your care. Chronic illness or disability—which, please note, are not automatically synonymous—change daily life so significantly that primary identity may shift to become mostly that.

In the world of Christianity, baptism transforms and distinguishes you as part of Christian community, but your identity will shift a bit (or a lot) if you become active in church leadership or seek ordination.

As for identity itself, you're better off thinking in terms of multiple identities and viewing them through the lens of sociology. From a sociological perspective, multiple identities are the predictable outcome of having multiple social statuses. Refusing to get stuck in any one achieved identity can be evidence of adaptability rather than avoidance or pathology.[1]

Point of Clarification:
Social Identity and Personal Identity

Defining and exploring identity has captured the attention of social scientists. Psychologists as well as sociologists acknowledge the impact of social interaction on identity development.

- *Social Identity:* Sociologists distinguish between ascribed and achieved identity. *Ascribed Identity:* Fixed at birth (e.g., race and ethnicity). *Achieved Identity:* Externally assigned or acquired as a result of behaviors/activities (e.g., parent, minister, scholar). *Role Strain:* When the expected roles (i.e., behaviors) of social identities collide.

- *Personal Identity:* Psychologists view personal identity as a mashup of all aspects of an individual's self (e.g., values, beliefs, attitudes, emotions, personality). *Cognitive Dissonance:* When perceptions about aspects of self collide.

Identity might be formed early on, but exploring and redefining it is a lifelong process. Or, depending on your attitude and outlook, it's a lifelong adventure. You'll try on, wear, and discard several identities throughout your life. Almost everyone does. I certainly have, and I'm not planning to stop anytime soon. Not for nothing do I characterize myself as having a multiple spirituality disorder. My LinkedIn profile reads like a catalog of occupations and professions.

In addition, just about everyone spends some percentage of time wondering about identity; more so when committed to self-discovery or forced into it by an identity crisis. During life transitions, some people focus on asking, "Who am I?" Others spend more time wondering, "How do others view me?" In either case, the questions are easy; the answers more complex and involve:

- *Exploring assumptions about identity.* What messages did you receive about who you should become? Who delivered those messages? Which messages about identity have you willingly and perhaps happily accepted? Which assumptions about identity—yours or others'—are you ready to challenge?

- *Dealing with disconnects.* Is your internal sense of self in alignment with the external identity you project? Do you comply with external rules that feel energy-and-soul sucking? Do you have the skills to manage whatever dissonance is unavoidable?

- *Seeking support for doing the work of identity.* Have you created a network of friends interested in and excited by exploring identity? Do you have and/or know where to find professional help when (or before) self-discovery becomes painful? Do you know when and how to avoid naysayers?

Identity Crisis according to Erik Erikson and James E. Marcia

Erik Erikson used the term "identity crisis" to describe a key developmental aspect of adolescence (see chapter 2: Exploring Psychosocial Development). Within decades, psychologists would acknowledge how everyone faces crises of identity (i.e., challenges to sense of self) throughout adulthood.[2] Life happens!

Developmental psychologist James E. Marcia explained shifts and changes in identity as normative. Whether someone uses crisis as an opportunity for growth is another issue.[3]

Marcia's Phases (Not Sequential Stages) of Identity Achievement Status[4]

Phase I: Identity Foreclosure
    Commitment to identity ascribed/conferred by others without exploring options.

Phase II: Identity Diffusion
No commitment to an identity nor any interest in exploring it.

Phase III: Identity Moratorium
Commitment to identity in flux and options are actively explored.

Phase IV: Identity Achievement
Commitment to identity because options have been explored and the identity crisis has been resolved—until the next one.

Knowing that your identity isn't fixed for all time is welcomed information, yes? Social science provides frameworks for understanding the answers that emerge during a wholehearted and open-minded exploration of identity. But what about the process itself?

Your understanding will be enriched by having conversations with others about identity conferred, embraced, rejected, and possibly revived. We cannot do this work of self alone. To prevent being stuck in a continuous loop of existential angst, we simply must invite and welcome help from others. More is always being revealed, especially when younger and older adults explore identity together.

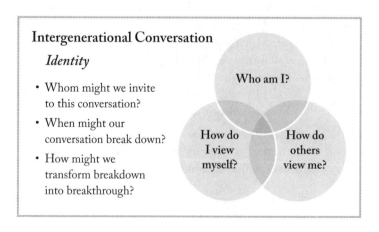

Intergenerational Conversation

Identity

- Whom might we invite to this conversation?

- When might our conversation break down?

- How might we transform breakdown into breakthrough?

Who am I?

How do I view myself?

How do others view me?

Exploring the Challenges of Identity

Perhaps you've already encountered the "Who am I" exercise if you took Sociology 101. This exercise is trotted out to help students understand what sociologists mean by social status(es)—that is, social position not prestige—and role(s)—that is, behaviors expected relative to those social statuses. Here it is again, as it's worth revisiting every five to ten years. New to you? Then have some illuminating (maybe) fun. Try this:

- Create a list with eighteen numbered lines.[5] Not kidding—number the lines *in advance*. You could do this on a computer but physically writing this, if you're able, will have more impact.

- For each and every consecutive line write your spontaneous first thought response to the question, "Who am I?"

Finish the list. If you run out of spontaneous answers, write "?" on the blank lines. Done with all that? Breathe and relax and eat chocolate before continuing.

Next, review your list, noticing the sequence and the frequency with which you connect your current identity to:

- beliefs and faith
- church and other communities
- earning money
- education
- family relations
- friendship networks
- health and fitness
- living arrangements
- physicality
- residence
- values

Consider sharing the results of this exercise with your therapist or spiritual director.

Names are such a significant feature of identity that every spiritual tradition has a ritual for naming and renaming. Contemplate your name using these questions to spark intergenerational conversations within and beyond your immediate family:

- *Family Name:* How often have first and last names changed within your family? Why were they changed? How was your first name chosen? How have your thoughts and feelings about your name(s) changed over time? What do you like about your name? If you've thought about changing it, what would you change it to and would you do that legally?

- *Nicknames:* Which nicknames have you had during your life? Why did those nicknames emerge? Which nicknames do you like? Which nicknames from the past have you kept secret from people in your present life—and why is that?!?

- *Titles:* Which titles or honorifics do you routinely use to identify yourself? When do you opt-out of using titles or honorifics? When do you insist that others use your title or honorific? When do you always use someone's title or honorific? How does that change if communication is written rather than verbal?

Time for a reality check about self-identity! Do what Jesus did and ask a few friends: "Who do you say that I am?" (Matt 16:15). After listening to their responses, gather more details by asking how they view you:

- relative to the secular world and world of church;

- in one-to-one situations and group settings, especially on teams or committees;

- when you know that others are watching; and

- when you think no one is paying attention to what you're doing or how you're being.

After gathering this intel, sort through it. Notice what is and what isn't in alignment with what you hope is true. For disconnects and especially any shockers, what steps will you take to get your insides aligned with your presentation of self in everyday life?[6] Who will you turn to for help with this?

The (Identity) Rite Stuff

Throughout history and across cultures, societies have developed rites of passage. These formal rituals acknowledge, reinforce, and celebrate changes in individual as well as community-shaped identity.

Baptism is a rite of passage to Christian identity; First Communion deepens that identity. Confirmation, a rite of passage typically occurring during middle school years, transforms individuals into members of a faith community. The Catholic Order of Christian Funerals includes the rite of committal celebrating final release from corporeal existence.

While not a religious ritual per se, the Hispanic community's Quinceanera celebration for girls at age 15 begins with renewing baptismal vows during Mass and special blessings by a priest or deacon.[7] The Amish community designates age 16 for starting Rumspringa, a time to explore the secular world up until age 26, before returning (or not) to become baptized members of the Amish church.

According to anthropologists, rites of passage involve: (1) severance—that is, preparing to leave everyone and everything behind; (2) threshold—that is, the time and space between old and new identity; and (3) incorporation—that is, returning to and becoming more identified with community.

Anthropologists also note how initiation rites typically involve ordeals, as well as celebrations, something to keep in mind as you plan a party for any rite of passage.

 ## Your Reality Check-Up: Identity

Contemplate your current reality and move forward by discussing:

- When have I been most interested and/or concerned about who I am?

- Who or what has best supported my search for identity?

- How might my faith community become a safe place to explore spiritual and secular identities?

Let's Get Biblical—Identity

Identity Created
- God created humankind in his image.
  (Gen 1:27)
- You are my Son, the Beloved; with you I am well pleased.
  (Mark 1:11)

Identity Revised
- No longer shall your name be Abram, but your name
  shall be Abraham, for I have made you the ancestor of
  a multitude of nations. (Gen 17:5)
- As for Sarai your wife, you shall not call her Sarai, but
  Sarah shall be her name. . . . She shall give rise to nations. (Gen 17:15-16)
- You shall no longer be called Jacob, but Israel, for you
  have striven with God and with humans, and have pre-
  vailed. (Gen 32:28)

Identity Recognized
- For the Lord does not see as mortals see; they look on
  the outward appearance, but the Lord looks on the heart.
  (1 Sam 16:7).
- You are the Messiah, the Son of the living God. (Matt
  16:16)
- You are Peter, and on this rock I will build my church.
  (Matt 16:18)

Reminders About Identity
- You are dust and to dust you shall return. (Gen 3:19)
- You are a people holy to the Lord your God; the Lord
  your God has chosen you out of all the people on earth
  to be his people. (Deut 7:6)
- Do not fear, for I have redeemed you; I have called you
  by name, you are mine. (Isa 43:1)
- You are the salt of the earth. . . . the light of the world.
  (Matt 5:13-14)

CHAPTER 6
Purpose

When did *you* last set aside some time to contemplate life's purpose? For some of us this search for meaning is a favorite sport. Everyone else typically waits to be forced by circumstances do this work of self. Something happens or doesn't. Feeling like something is missing becomes too persistent to ignore. Someone asks when you plan to get it together or gently invites you to take a break from [distraction of your choice] to explore your immediate and future purpose. Me? I contemplate my life's purpose every time I write a book, which just underscores my point about being forced by circumstances—but also about it being a sport.

The key question for excavating life's purpose is, of course, "Why am I here?" As they will when you explore identity, your answers will be shaped by the timing of and context for inquiry. Are you questioning your life's purpose two years after graduating from high school? Two years after graduating from college? Two years after retiring from a job that turned into a career? Are you wondering about existence while struggling to pay rent? While living on an inheritance? While focusing on fulfilling what Abraham Maslow characterized as "esteem needs"?

Purpose and Meaning according to
Abraham Maslow

Psychologist Abraham Maslow (1908–70) is everyone's go-to theorist when it comes to understanding human motivation and potential. Maslow argued that people have basic needs that, once met, motivate a search to fulfill psychosocial ones. Only after psychosocial needs are satisfied do we become motivated to achieve self-actualization. Maslow emphasized how this is an ongoing process.[1]

During the 1960s, Maslow added transcendence needs (i.e., helping others to achieve self-actualization) after self-actualization. The 1970 edition of *Motivation and Personality* placed cognitive and aesthetic needs between esteem needs and self-actualization.[2] Note: although Maslow's five-stage model is depicted as a pyramid-shaped hierarchy, he did not present it that way in his original work (1954).

Maslow's Hierarchy of Needs (Basic Five-Stage Version)

Basic Needs
   Level I: Physiological Needs
      air, water, food, clothing, shelter, sleep, sex
   Level II: Safety and Security Needs
      order, stability, certainty, routine, familiarity, protection
      from fear and disease, physical safety, economic security,
      freedom from threat

Psychosocial Needs
   Level III: Social Needs
      love, acceptance, belonging, affection
   Level IV: Esteem Needs
      respect and recognition from others, self-respect, a sense
      of prestige, independence, achievement, mastery

Self-Fulfillment Needs
  Level V: Self-Actualization Needs
    "peak" experiences, fulfilling a sense of self and calling,
    opportunities for learning and creating at higher levels

How you articulate the question will shift during transitions from one life stage to another (reread chapter 2: Exploring Psychosocial Development). Questioning purpose during young adulthood generally turns into wondering about shifting focus as middle age approaches. During the fifth decade of life, we tend to question whether it's too late to focus on something else. (Spoiler Alert: The answer is, "No, it's rarely ever too late to focus on something else.") Asking "Was *that* really my focus?" when Medicare eligibility kicks in could be the impetus to rediscover and redefine purpose.

Frame the question about your life's purpose in spiritual terms and notice how this inquiry shifts from head to heart; to within and beyond.

Purpose is more easily discovered by paying attention to how belief informs values. You believe in God's infinite grace; and so, you value generosity. You've taken to heart Jesus of Nazareth's reminder about making disciples of all nations; and so, you value teachers and teaching. You believe in welcoming the Other; and so, you value social justice.

Seeking *God's* will is radically different from wondering what *you* should be doing to live a meaningful life.[3] Asking "What is God's will for my life?" moves spiritual gifts from background to foreground as strengths to be discerned and shared. When career is experienced as vocation, hearing a small, still voice say, "Well done, good and faithful servant" (Matt 25:21, NIV) is more meaningful than scoring high marks on a 360 review.[4]

But even if you've discovered your life's purpose, these questions about getting to that glorious destination still remain to be asked and answered:

- *How will I get there?* Are you doing the necessary and ongoing work of identity? What lifestyle changes must you make to align your values with your life's purpose? Will you need to change careers? Learn how to stick to a budget? Have you defined fulfillment in ways that no longer make sense?

- *Who will guide me?* Who are your role models? Have you chosen role models who have become measuring sticks with which you smack yourself? Do you know how to distinguish among types of guidance? Can you recognize when you resist counsel?

- *Who are my companions?* Have you gotten bogged down in thinking that exploring life's purpose is a solo endeavor? Are you willing to set aside age- or generation-based assumptions to increase the number of fellow travelers on your journey?

Surprise no surprise, once again, you've entered the domain of lifelong inquiry, discovery, and rediscovery.[5]

Conversations about life's purpose with adults of all ages will swiftly reveal how you're not the only one feeling like a work in regress rather than a work in progress. Faith community conversations about life's purpose are especially valuable when secular markers for achievement, success, fulfillment, and meaning no longer make sense. And if an invitation to find your "passion" seems more inspiring than one to discover your "purpose," then use the snazzier word, especially if it enhances collaboration.

Point of Clarification:
Job, Career, and Vocation

Just about everyone claims to know how to distinguish a job from a career, and career from vocation—and then confuses the terms. To be fair, confusion sometimes stems from understanding when and how a job might turn into a career, as well as an unwillingness to acknowledge when vocation has devolved into a job.

Jobs entail work that:
- involves earning money;
- may not align with personal values; and
- feels like an obligation.

Careers entail work that:
- involves choice and opportunities;
- usually aligns with personal values; and
- feels like a (energizing or devitalizing) challenge.

Vocations entail work that:
- involves being and doing;
- aligns with personal values; and
- feels like being called by God.

The word "vocation" is rooted in the Latin *vocare* (to call). Catholics use "vocation" when referring to serving in the priesthood or religious life. Protestants tend to refer to ministry as a "call."

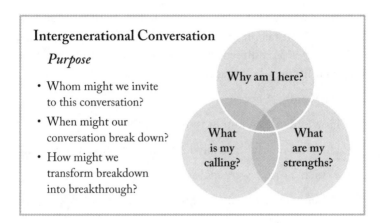

Intergenerational Conversation

Purpose

- Whom might we invite to this conversation?
- When might our conversation break down?
- How might we transform breakdown into breakthrough?

Why am I here?

What is my calling?

What are my strengths?

Exploring the Challenges of Purpose

Challenge your current sense of purpose while discovering hidden values by completing these sentences, preferably by writing them out in a notebook created for this—purpose:

"I'll be happy when _____ ."

"I'll know I've accomplished something when _____ ."

"Everyone I respect and trust tells me I should _____ ."

"I get stuck when _____ ."

"If there were absolutely no barriers, I would _____ ."

What do your answers reveal? What can you change? What's beyond your control? What depends on other people's involvement? What seems contingent on chronological age, psychosocial development, or generational cohort? What seems connected to your religious beliefs and/or spiritual commitments?

Gain insight about fulfilling your life's purpose by interviewing one or two people you aspire to be like *and* who are older than you by *at least* fifteen years. You want to seek and find your imagined future self and ask:

- How did you become who you are?

- How did you end up in your career?

- How has your faith factored into your choices and decisions?

- Which barriers were most unexpected?

- Which detours turned out to be the most valuable?

- What would you have done differently?

Most people respond warmly to authentic requests for this type of help and love talking about themselves, so don't worry about being a nuisance. If coffee and/or food is involved, plan to pick up the tab for it. Also consider taping the conversation— asking permission to do so, of course!

Given the known links between personality and career choice, revisit the following well-known and credible assessments. Searching Google will lead to online self-assessments for personality and career.[6] Also consider getting your personality assessment administered and analyzed by a trained professional. Explore in yet more depth by taking a workshop about one or more of these tools:

- *Myers–Briggs Type Indicator® (MBTI®):* Developed in the 1940s and first published in 1962, the MBTI is anchored in Carl Jung's theory of personality.

- *The Enneagram of Personality:* Original specific provenance in dispute but just about everyone agrees that early twentieth-century mystic Gurdjieff deserves credit.

- *Strong Interest Inventory® (SII):* Originally published in 1927 and has evolved over time to measure General Occupational Themes (GOTs), Basic Interest Scales (BISs), Personal Style Scales (PSSs), and Occupational Scales (OSs).

- *The MAPP™ Career Assessment:* Launched in 1994 as a 400-question written career test and now online as a 71-question test.

Keep in mind (how could you not?) that spiritual gifts (a.k.a. charisms of the Holy Spirit) are also a factor. Typing "spiritual gifts assessment" into the search bar will yield an abundance of resources from across denominations.[7]

Gather results and contemplate whether there's anything you'd like to rethink or swiftly change about your life's purpose. Revisit these tests periodically to discover what might have changed over time.

 ## Your Reality Check-Up: Purpose

Contemplate your current reality and move forward by discussing:

- How and why has my sense of purpose changed over the years?

- When have I been most likely to shift my focus to seeking God's will for my life?

- Who in my faith community illuminates and supports my sense of purpose?

Let's Get Biblical—Purpose

Purpose Questioned
- And now, O Lord, what do I wait for? My hope is in you. (Ps 39:7)
- Why did I come forth from the womb to see toil and sorrow? (Jer 20:18)

Purpose Revealed
- But this is why I have let you live: to show you my power, and to make my name resound through all the earth. (Exod 9:16)
- For everything there is a season, and a time for every matter under heaven. (Eccl 3:1)[8]
- So shall my word be that goes out from my mouth; it shall not return to me empty, but it shall accomplish that which I purpose. (Isa 55:11)
- For we are what he has made us, created in Christ Jesus for good works. (Eph 2:10)

Purpose Designated
- For the Lord your God has chosen Levi out of all your tribes, to stand and minister in the name of the Lord. (Deut 18:5)
- The human mind may devise many plans, but it is the purpose of the Lord that will be established. (Prov 19:21)
- Whatever town or village you enter, find out who in it is worthy, and stay there until you leave. (Matt 10:11)
- We know that all things work together for good for those who love God, who are called according to his purpose. (Rom 8:28)

God's Purpose Accepted—Sometimes Grudgingly

- I know that you can do all things, and that no purpose of yours can be thwarted. (Job 42:2)
- For there is still a vision for the appointed time; it speaks of the end, and does not lie. If it seems to tarry, wait for it; it will surely come, it will not delay. (Hab 2:3)

CHAPTER 7
Belonging

We make such a big deal about how faith is lived in and enhanced by community. Far too often, however, our assertions have little to do with people feeling as if they belong. In this instance, "we" refers to people of faith who congregate within the institution known as "church," and "we" don't like to acknowledge this reality. Maybe this truth will soften that sting: no matter which stage of adulthood you're waltzing or trudging through or which generational cohort you claim as your own, you're in good company if you sometimes—or often—feel like an outsider.[1]

Let there be comfort in knowing that you're not the only one asking if and where you belong. Nor are you the only one wondering if you ever belonged when any belongingness you once experienced fades. Your feelings are not unique because the need to belong is a culturally universal human need. Even those who can't, don't, or won't fit in end up creating communities of misfits (a.k.a. countercultures).

Belonging according to
Roy F. Baumeister and Mark R. Leary

Abraham Maslow's characterization of belonging as a psychosocial need had been long
accepted by the time Roy F. Baumeister (1953–) and Mark R.
Leary (1954–) proposed the "belongingness hypothesis." Their
widely cited journal article provided a foundation for understanding an entire body of research and theory about human
motivation.[2]

Good news: belongingness drives us to seek new relationships
when existing ones end.

Bad news: belongingness can undermine our ability to end
dysfunctional relationships. Note: relationships can be one-to-
one or one-with-a-group.[3]

Baumeister and Leary's Criteria for Satisfying the Need to Belong
Interactions must be:

- frequent *and* pleasant *or* positive;
- with the *same* individuals;
- involve a *minimum* number of social contacts;
- within a long-term *and* stable framework;
- personal *and* meaningful;
- reveal *and* support mutual care *and* concern; and
- provide social feedback like validation.

Message from The Duh Department: Attitudes and expectations about belonging are shaped by experience.

Almost everyone's first experience of belonging happens within
a family. Anyone growing up in a ginormous family learns about
pecking order, distribution of labor, and resource management.
Those growing up in blended families learn the dynamics of inclusion and exclusion, challenges of cooperation, and how to accommodate different traditions, especially within interfaith ones.

Those held hostage in dysfunctional families sometimes (please, dear God) learn about belonging from healthier adults in their lives as teachers, social workers, therapists, and ministers. Growing up in a household with multiple generations helps members learn what fosters or undermines intergenerational respect.

Everything Old Is New Again: Intergenerational Living

Intergenerational households were commonplace for centuries. They went out of style during the mid-twentieth century for families that could afford to take advantage of the post–World War II single family housing boom. By 2010, demographers were announcing the resurgence of intergenerational living, crediting young adults for this trend.[4]

It looks like what may have been driven by economic necessity is developing into a lifestyle choice. Members of multigenerational households seem to be recognizing the social and health benefits of social support.[5] Note: intergenerational living can refer to households comprising blood relations and those brought together by friendship or other commitments. Religious communities are also an example of multigenerational living.

The belonging cultivated by peers early on, especially now that pre-preschool programs exist, is further reinforced by peers during adolescence. Under the best of circumstances, friends help us experience belonging as we develop identity (see chapter 5: Identity). During young adulthood, peer influence shifts from playgrounds to conference rooms. By middle adulthood, attitudes about age and generations have become more deeply rooted and bloomed as behavior (see chapter 4: A Bit about Stereotypes and Ageism). Nevertheless, belonging—the desire for or lack thereof—remains an issue. What shifts throughout adulthood is the *context* for asking: Where do I belong? How do I belong? Who are my people?

Point of Clarification:
Group and Community

Every community is a group but not all groups become communities. Distinguishing between these social units should help you understand the dynamics of belonging. Note: definitions apply whether the social unit emerges in person or online.[6]

Group: Collection of individuals with characteristics in common that influence attitudes, beliefs, behavior, and personality. Primary groups include family and friends. Secondary groups, which can be larger and/or temporary, include those created to focus on work, study, or hobbies. Kinship is also a term used for social groups organized by genetic origins as well as rituals (e.g., marriage) or socially constructed relationships (e.g., adoption).

Community: Group that shares beliefs, values, interests, needs, skills, and goals, actively encouraging and supporting members.[7] Healthy communities provide members emotional connection within a safe space. Communities are likely to split or dissolve completely when dissonant values and dissident behaviors emerge.

The core question, "Where do I belong?" typically emerges when young adults leave the community-driven environment of college and enter the competitive environment of work. Middle-age adults start wondering where they belong when playdates, carpooling, and school sports dissolve as the glue holding together a community of parents. Older adults in their final decades of life may drift into social isolation and perhaps desolation as same-age friends and colleagues die.[8] These examples and the many more that you can easily imagine underscore how belonging is not only a feeling but also an action.

Belongingness requires the individual as well as the community to:

- *Connect:* Which barriers to connection are real or imagined? How much freedom and safety is there to reveal all aspects of self? When do personal privacy needs turn into social isolation behavior? When does the human need to connect turn into neediness?

- *Accept:* How much diversity among community members is welcomed? Tolerated? What are the mechanisms of inclusion? How are divergent viewpoints received? How are diverging needs accommodated? Must acceptance mean agreement? What are the dynamics of exclusion?

- *Participate:* Are there enough opportunities for individuals to participate? How does contributing to the community supersede serving self? How do structures of community authority affect participation?

So now what about our communities of faith? Your congregation?

Our first impulse is to claim that church is, by definition, a community that promotes belongingness. We like to think shared belief eclipses demographics and have collectively constructed church culture to affirm that. Some examples: Since 1994, Roman Catholic parishes have enthusiastically sung a hymn about building "a house where love can dwell and all can safely live" and how "all are welcome in this place."[9] You can easily find church marquees and publications inviting everyone to become part of "our church family."[10] At least one Protestant denomination has a universally recognized tagline asserting that it "welcomes you."

But saying it, singing it, or erecting signage claiming that any church is a place to belong, doesn't make it so, especially when assumptions about age and generation-based interaction persist. Collaboration in the world of church becomes possible when adults of all ages are willing, able, and safe to discuss their longing for belonging.

On Being Terminally Unique

Among the many contributions of Twelve Step recovery is the notion of "terminal uniqueness," a term that underscores the dangers of clinging to personal exceptionalism. Within the context of addiction recovery, this tendency to view oneself as extraordinarily special is considered a form of denial.

But you don't have to be in denial about addiction to get invested in terminal uniqueness; the concept is useful for understanding how individuals unconsciously opt out of belonging. Consider, too, how claiming and clinging to the uniqueness of an entire generation might undermine collaboration.

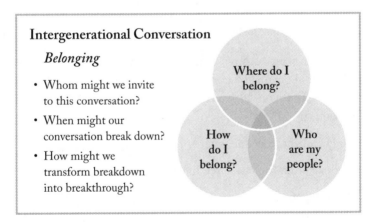

Intergenerational Conversation

Belonging

- Whom might we invite to this conversation?

- When might our conversation break down?

- How might we transform breakdown into breakthrough?

Where do I belong?

How do I belong?

Who are my people?

Exploring Challenges of Belonging

You've joined many groups during your life, now make time to examine them through the microscope lens of belonging. To get started, list all the clubs, groups, and organizations you can remember joining over the years. Go ahead and start with

Brownies or Cub Scouts, include your high school marching band and college sorority or fraternity as well as civic and church organizations.[11]

After finishing the list, hunker down to write out your gut response to these questions for *each* group:

- Why did I join?

- What did belonging mean to me at the time?

- Why and when did I leave? (If you're still a member, then ponder why and when you might opt out.)

Consider sharing the results of this exercise with your therapist or spiritual director.

Discover your automatic thoughts about belonging to intergenerational groups by completing these sentences, preferably by writing them out by hand so that your body literally connects with your mind:

"I only feel comfortable when _____ ."

"I believe older members see me as _____ ."

"I believe younger members see me as _____ ."

"I'm afraid that younger members will _____ ."

"I'm afraid that older members will _____ ."[12]

What do your answers reveal? What could you do to reduce or eliminate fears about intergenerational groups? What could the group do to reveal and deal with barriers to belonging?

Enhance your felt sense of belonging to a larger community of faith by setting aside an entire year to live in sync with the liturgical calendar—consciously! Let the flow of holy seasons and celebrations supplement secular ones by doing some or all of the following:

- Go beyond recording dates for liturgical seasons on your calendar by noting the liturgical colors as well.[13]

- Surround yourself with visual reminders by changing home and office decorations to reflect liturgical colors and symbols.

- Learn about and observing historically ethnic or folk traditions for celebrating holy days and seasons.[14]

- Listen to seasonally specific sacred music. ProTip: Find playlists by searching YouTube and/or Spotify or create your own!

Bonus points—and spiritual growth—by expanding your belongingness by learning more about "appointed feasts of the Lord" according to Jewish law (i.e., Torah).[15]

Your Reality Check-Up: Belonging

Contemplate your current reality and move forward by discussing:

- How and why might I exclude or remove myself from belonging?

- When would I actively seek participation in an inter-generational group?

- How does faith illuminate and support my sense of belonging within and beyond church-the-building?

Let's Get Biblical—Belonging

Belonging to God

- Rise up, O God, judge the earth; for all the nations belong to you! (Ps 82:8)

- For all things are yours . . . all belong to you, and you belong to Christ, and Christ belongs to God. (1 Cor 3:21-23)

Belonging Celebrated

- O Lord, I love the house in which you dwell, and the place where your glory abides. (Ps 26:8)

- You who live in the shelter of the Most High, who abide in the shadow of the Almighty, will say to the Lord, "My refuge and my fortress; my God, in whom I trust." (Ps 91:1-2)

- How very good and pleasant it is when kindred live together in unity! (Ps 133:1)

- I was hungry and you gave me food, I was thirsty and you gave me drink, I was a stranger and you welcomed me. (Matt 25:35)
- Welcome one another, therefore, just as Christ has welcomed you, for the glory of God. (Rom 15:7)

Reminders about Belonging

- I will dwell among the Israelites, and I will be their God. (Exod 29:45)
- When an alien resides with you in your land, you shall not oppress the alien. (Lev 19:33)
- You shall also love the stranger, for you were strangers in the land of Egypt. (Deut 10:19)
- Because you have made the Lord your refuge, the Most High your dwelling place, no evil shall befall you, no scourge come near your tent. (Ps 91:9-10)
- Two are better than one, because they have a good reward for their toil. For if they fall, one will lift up the other; but woe to one who is alone and falls and does not have another to help. (Eccl 4:9-10)
- Whoever welcomes you welcomes me, and whoever welcomes me welcomes the one who sent me. (Matt 10:40)
- For where two or three are gathered in my name, I am there among them. (Matt 18:20)

CHAPTER 8
Legacy

Legacy might seem like a super grown-up and approaching end-of-life concern, but really it isn't. Since legacy involves bequeathing values as well as tangible assets, legacy building should (yes, should!) be attended to throughout adulthood.

Wanting life to have enduring meaning is radically tied to the search for identity, purpose, and belonging throughout adulthood. Even if we don't articulate it as legacy building we wonder about making a mark and whether our life matters, especially during seasons of transition. Notice how many of these examples resonate with your experience:

- Your family moved while you were in elementary or high school. At times you wonder if and how those playmates, classmates, and teammates remember you.

- You've changed jobs or perhaps entire careers multiple times throughout adulthood. You hope you've made a long-lasting positive impression and memorable contributions.

- Unto you a child or children, grandchild or grandchildren are born or become part of your family by other ways and means. You start getting serious about creating a testamentary will.

- Your oh-so-very-interesting life has included screwing up and cleaning up. To provide insight and impart what you've learned you begin writing an ethical will.

- You or loved ones have a life-threatening or chronic illness, or perhaps a life-altering disability. You decide to revise your living will to ensure your quality of life as well as the quality of your inevitable death.

Point of Clarification:
Testamentary Will, Living Will,
and Ethical Will

You've built or are building your legacy. How will you convey it? Legal means are complicated by differences in state law. Similarities among the terms used for managing life before and after death are confusing. Add reemerging interest in nonlegal testaments, and it's easy to understand why people avoid dealing with legacy transmission.

- *Testamentary Will:* Legal document detailing how money, property, and other tangible assets will be distributed after your death. Also identifies who will serve as your estate's legal representative. Create when: assets start accumulating. Also known as: a will/last will and testament.

- *Living Will:* Legal document specifying medical treatments you want when you can no longer make those decisions. Create when: legally able to do so and long before needing it. Also known as: a health care declaration/medical directive.[1] Not to be confused with: durable power of attorney for health care/health care proxy/health care surrogate/patient advocate designation, all of which refer to granting someone complete legal authority to make medical decisions if you become incapacitated.[2]

- *Ethical Will:* Personal document for sharing values, beliefs, ethics, key experiences, treasured memories, challenges faced, as well as life instructions for loved ones after your death. May include genealogical information and family stories as well as confessions and apologies. Not a legal document. Create when: you've finished learning all about it! Also known as: a legacy letter.[3]

If you need more proof of multigenerational interest in legacy, you'll find plenty by reviewing what your friends post to Facebook. Those #TBT (Throwback Thursday) posts? They're the family photos shared with a far-flung community instead of being tossed into boxes for the next generation to sort through. Those baby pictures? Ooh and aah, click "love" instead of "like," and then make time to study the comments. Here I'm thinking about my own gasp of recognition upon seeing the picture of a friend's (beyond adorable) first grandson. But wait, it gets better. Scrolling through the comments I saw this one from my friend's son, "He looks exactly like grandpa!" Legacy recognized and acknowledged. Notice how the quantity and quality of interactions change as class reunions approach. And those are just a few examples of how legacy is memorialized with online digital tools. The fact that social media platforms have created protocols for digital legacy planning underscores our desire to let people know who we are and what we've accomplished.[4]

Legacy in the Digital Age

For most of human history, evidence of existence was carved into cave walls, recorded on clay tablets and in diaries; shared through storytelling and letters that, before the telephone was invented, were written and delivered throughout the day. When the World Wide Web was created in 1990 this changed for everyone, not just "Digital Natives."

Today's Internet users maintain dozens of online accounts to manage daily life, separate from social networking platforms.[5] Digital estate planning has become enough of a thing to prompt the Uniform Law Commission to release a revised version of the Uniform Fiduciary Access to Digital Assets Act (UFADAA) in 2015.[6]

Until Facebook took the lead, social media platforms either allowed accounts to continue unaltered and unmonitored after the user's death or removed them entirely after receiving official notification. In 2014, Facebook changed its privacy settings so a memorialized profile could function as originally set up by the deceased user. Facebook added a "legacy contact" feature in 2015 so users could designate someone to manage their digital legacy.[7] Make a note to get that handled when you take a break from reading this book.

Meanwhile in the domain of face-to-face interaction, some families assiduously avoid discussing legacy, fearing that doing so will come across as morbid self-absorption.[8] Their fear is well founded because most people in the United States would rather talk about almost anything—including sexuality—than mortality. Pretty much impossible to talk about legacy without talking about dying and death, right?

Belief in eternal life seems to make discussing death only nominally tolerable for Christians, which makes intergenerational conversations about legacy challenging, but not impossible. Where to begin?

Start by viewing legacy building not as a gruesome preoccupation but an extension of living and sharing your life's purpose. This conscious reframe should make it somewhat easier to share thoughts and feelings about how you want to be remembered. Actively create safe spaces for conversation. Cultivate your listening skills. Invite people younger and older (not necessarily and probably not family members) to join the conversation about leaving a legacy that reflects life lived with the assurance of things hoped for and the conviction of things not seen (Heb 11:1). In other words, living a life of faith that will be remembered for how belief guided ethical action.[9]

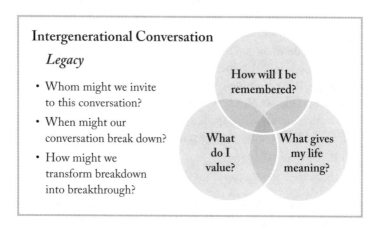

Exploring the Challenges of Legacy

Leaving a legacy begins with developing more clarity about what your legacy will include. Begin by generating a list of characteristics and accomplishments for which you hope to be warmly remembered after departing this mortal coil.

Start by:

- titling a page, "I want to be remembered for . . .";

- creating a list with 18 numbered lines;[10] and

- filling in those lines with specifics about your contributions to family (immediate and extended), community (sacred, secular, face-to-face, online), and your world of work.

Next, review your list and rank your hoped-for legacy items in order of importance. After completing that, take a brief break to let it all sink in but *do* return. Thinking about legacy is not the same as doing something about it!

Study your rank ordered list.

Anything need to be removed? Added? How do your best intentions align with current actions and activities? What will you need to change? Who or what will support your efforts? When and how will you move forward to ensure your legacy? Write it all down! Develop a timeline for action and configure digital reminders. No one is too young or too old to create a legacy.

Contemplative writing! Get out a journal and a pen or pencil for this, setting aside uninterrupted quiet time to interact with these questions.

To identify what you want loved ones to learn about your spiritual life:

- Which spiritual practices have had the most meaning and value?

- How have you cultivated your sense of the divine?

- What has supported your sense of mystery?

To identify what you want loved ones to learn about your religious life:

- Which Scripture stories and verses have provided the most guidance?

- How have religious beliefs shaped your secular life?

- Which religious beliefs have been the most challenging?

To identify what you want loved ones to learn about your relationship with church:

- When has church community had the most meaning and value?

- How have you managed disappointments with the institutional church?

- Which forms of participation have supported your faith?

Use your answers to have an intergenerational conversation and/or to craft part of a legacy letter.

Locate your hoped-for legacy within the human family by having a conversation about legacy with people older (by at least fifteen years) *and* younger (by at most ten years) than you, asking:

- At this age and stage of your life, for what would you most like to be remembered—
  - by family?
  - by friends?
  - by colleagues?
  - by sacred and secular community?
  - How have you changed what you'd like to be remembered for over the years?
  - Who or what has caused or contributed to changes in how you think about your legacy?
  - To what extent does your legacy feel like a work in progress? What would make it feel complete?

- At *this point in time*, for what and how will you be remembered—
  - by family?
  - by friends?
  - by colleagues?
  - by sacred and secular community?

As a practical matter, this conversation could happen within an intergenerational group but consider (also) having individual conversations. Bonus points for interviewing people you have already interviewed about their life's purpose.

 Your Reality Check-Up: Legacy

Contemplate your current reality and move forward by discussing:

- When have I been most concerned about my legacy?

- Which aspects of my legacy am I currently building?

- How does faith shape my aspirations for legacy?

Let's Get Biblical—Legacy

Legacy Assured

- I call heaven and earth to witness against you today that I have set before you life and death, blessings and curses. Choose life so that you and your descendants may live. (Deut 30:19)

- The Lord knows the days of the blameless, and their heritage will abide forever. (Ps 37:18)

- Train children in the right way, and when old, they will not stray. (Prov 22:6)

- All your children shall be taught by the Lord, and great shall be the prosperity of your children. (Isa 54:13)

- In Christ we have also obtained an inheritance, having been destined according to the purpose of him who accomplishes all things according to his counsel and will, so that we, who were the first to set our hope on Christ, might live for the praise of his glory. (Eph 1:11-12)

Reminders About Legacy

- You shall love the Lord your God with all your heart, and with all your soul, and with all your might. Keep these words that I am commanding you today in your heart. Recite them to your children and talk about them when you are at home and when you are away, when you lie down and when you rise. (Deut 6:5-7) [11]

- We will not hide them from their children; we will tell to the coming generation the glorious deeds of the Lord, and his might, and the wonders that he has done. (Ps 78:4)

- One generation shall laud your works to another, and shall declare your mighty acts. (Ps 145:4)

- The good leave an inheritance to their children's children. (Prov 13:22)

SECTION III
Moving Forward Together

Moving forward together involves learning and cultivating core skills. In this section, I focus on three of them: listening, decision-making, and embracing change.

CHAPTER 9
Listening

There is no shortage of ways to communicate within and beyond the world of church, and you can count on many more tools, especially digital ones, to emerge over time.[1] In the face of all this—and probably because of it—I've come to believe that listening is one of the least cultivated aspects of communication. And I do mean *listening*, which involves seeking to understand input, as opposed to *hearing*, merely the passive reception of sound.[2]

Many breakdowns in collaborative efforts can be traced to underdeveloped listening skills. Collaboration is also debilitated by weird assumptions about how people are supposed to listen and what listening should look like, especially if anyone is watching. Decision-making suffers as well, but I'll focus on that in the next chapter (see chapter 10: Decision-Making)

A Bit More about Hearing and Listening

During the 1950s, Dr. Alfred Tomatis (1920–2001), an Ear, Nose, and Throat specialist proposed that hearing (i.e., passively perceiving sound via the ear) and listening (that is, actively seeking to understand the meaning of sound) should be regarded as different albeit related functions.

Tomatis also made a case for the impact of hearing on voice production as well as speech and language. In addition, he asserted that hearing ability influenced motor skills and coordination. He developed the "Auditory Integration Technique" (a.k.a. the Tomatis Method) to improve ear–brain coordination.[3] Like any other therapeutic technique, the Tomatis Method has its critics, but enthusiasts seem to outnumber naysayers.

As for attributing lousy listening to members of any specific generation of adults, oh please just don't. Focus instead on learning more about listening as a core communication skill.

Begin by distinguishing among these five types of listening—informational, critical, relationship, sympathetic, and appreciative. Each type of listening has specific goals and focal points; all have identifiable impediments that undermine listening (see chart on p. 77: Types of Listening).

Next, knowing more about how people learn should help you become less judgmental and more generous about how others listen.[4] Those knitters, doodlers, smartphone users, and people with the fidgets are kinesthetic learners. The people who absolutely must have printed handouts and slides in advance of your presentation are visual learners. Those who keep asking you to repeat everything are either auditory learners or struggling with environmental obstacles to listening.

Accounting for listeners' dominant communication style will also help you understand and reinterpret what might seem like off-putting behaviors.[5] The person who listens with precious little patience is probably a "doer" who wants to move from conversation to action more quickly than you'd like. The person you swiftly dismiss as rude is probably an "influencer" whose interruptions come more from their excitement than disrespect. They are not going to change, so how will you help them listen?

You'll also need to understand and adjust whatever can be adjusted to enhance listening—yours and everyone else's. You may be up against some or all of the following deterrents:

Ecological:[6] Is the environment hampering your ability to listen? Are acoustics and/or the sound system so awful that you can't track voice tone or inflection? Are you sitting in rows (i.e., classroom style) that make it difficult to see speakers' nonverbal support (or lack thereof) for what they're saying? Are you distracted by other forms of sensory stimulation?

Linguistic: Do you tune out in the presence of slang, buzz-words, or in-group jargon? Do speech styles like upspeak or verbal tics like "uh" or "um" stop you from listening? Are you easily offended by irreverent, blunt speech, so-called bad or naughty words, and/or negative body language?[7] What assumptions do you make about how women and men listen? Note: Language is linguistic communication. Body posture, facial expressions, shrieking, and laughing are examples of nonlinguistic communication.[8]

Psychological: Did you feel "not heard" by family, peers, teachers, and/or faith leaders when growing up? Do you still feel that way? Are you entering situations already feeling angry, disgusted, confused, or defensive? Do you have so much alone time that all you can do is talk when you're finally around people? Do you know everything in advance or behave as if you do? Are you (secretly) afraid of being too stupid to understand? Are you too stressed to listen?[9] Do you know the difference between "can't listen" and "won't listen"?

Ecclesial: Do structures of church authority trigger resistance to listening? Do you mentally leave the sanctuary if a sermon is longer than 8.5 minutes?

Women, Men, and Listening

Robin Lakoff's sociolinguistic work in the 1970s and that of her student, Deborah Tannen, during the 1980s, highlighted differences in ways women and men speak. Lakoff identified ten speech elements women tend to use more frequently than men.[10] Tannen identified six main differences in how women and men use language.[11] She also introduced the term "Genderlect" to emphasize how female and male speech differences are better understood as different dialects of the same language.

Their work led more than a few people to conclude women are better listeners than men, but neither Lakoff nor Tannen argued this. Instead, they invited us to think more sociologically about *why* these differences emerged. Consider if and when speech elements named by Lakoff and language differences identified by Tannen would apply to intergenerational speaking and listening.

Communication specialists, including those with psychological, sociological, and linguistic training have identified effective tactics for overcoming barriers to listening. These tactics include but are not limited to:

- checking sound systems,

- rearranging seating,

- reconfiguring big groups into smaller ones,

- agreeing to ditch churchy church jargon,

- getting schooled about nonlinguistic communication,

- asking about or going online to discover what might be authentically generational idioms, and

- reducing internal and external stress with conscientious self-care.

Bookmark This: Urban Dictionary

Thanks to the creativity of an undergrad at Cal Poly (California Polytechnic State University), you can get swift intel about slang as well as generational and culturally specific phrases by consulting www.urbandictionary.com.

This crowd-sourced online compendium was developed by Aaron Peckham at the end of the twentieth century. Since then, millions of definitions have been added by users. Thousands of new entries are posted daily and now routinely used in court cases.[12] *Urban Dictionary* also has identified lingo that eventually made its way into traditional dictionaries. Make it your go-to resource to decipher culture-specific idioms and generational patois, but be cautious about using what you find to sound cool, hip, or awesomesauce.

Types of Listening			
	Goals	**Foci**	**Impediments**
Informational	Understanding and Learning	Facts and Details	Arrogance Unwillingness to Learn
Critical	Analyzing, Evaluating, and Responding	Meaning and Nuance	Biases Vocabulary Poor Analytic Skills
Relationship	Establishing and/or Deepening Rapport	Verbal and Non-verbal Clues	Distractibility Difficulty Maintaining Boundaries Lack of Empathy
Sympathetic	Understanding to Provide Support	Verbal and Non-verbal Clues	Distractibility Difficulty Maintaining Boundaries Already Established Agenda
Appreciative	Enjoyment	Sound Verbal and Non-verbal Clues	Lack of Access

Listening also involves willingness, curiosity, empathy, and generosity, so plan to embrace those spiritual practices of being. Of course, you'll need to do a lot more than "listen up" to foster collaboration, let alone enhance it. You'll need to learn how to listen with an open mind and heart, finding comfort in knowing that listening skills can deepen over time, especially when they're nurtured.

Your Reality Check-Up: Listening

Contemplate your current reality and move forward by discussing:

- When am I most likely to listen?

- Which situations and conditions are practically guaranteed to make me stop listening?

- Which listening skills do I need to develop, enhance, or resurrect?

Let's Get Biblical—Listening

Listening to God

- [The Lord] said, "If you will listen carefully to the voice of the Lord your God, and do what is right in his sight, and give heed to his commandments and keep all his statutes, I will not bring upon you any of the diseases that are brought upon the Egyptians." (Exod 15:26)

- Eli said to Samuel, "Go, lie down; and if he calls you, you shall say, 'Speak, Lord, for your servant is listening.'" So Samuel went and lay down in his place. Now the Lord came and stood there, calling as before, "Samuel! Samuel!" And Samuel said, "Speak, for your servant is listening." (1 Sam 3:9-10)

- While he was still speaking, suddenly a bright cloud overshadowed them, and from the cloud a voice said, "This is my Son, the Beloved; with him I am well pleased; listen to him!" (Matt 17:5)

Listening Questioned

- Then Moses answered, "But suppose they do not believe me or listen to me, but say, 'The Lord did not appear to you.'" (Exod 4:1)

- But Moses spoke to the Lord, "the Israelites have not listened to me; how then shall Pharaoh listen to me, poor speaker that I am?" (Exod 6:12)

- If I summoned him and he answered me, I do not believe that he would listen to my voice. (Job 9:16)

- Jesus said to them, "Why are you talking about having no bread? Do you still not perceive or understand? Are your hearts hardened? Do you have eyes, and fail to see? Do you have ears, and fail to hear? And do you not remember? (Mark 8:17-18)

Consequences of Not Listening

- But they did not listen to Moses; some left part of it until morning, and it bred worms and became foul. (Exod 16:20)
- For the Israelites traveled forty years in the wilderness, until all the nation, the warriors who came out of Egypt, perished, not having listened to the voice of the Lord. (Josh 5:6)
- But if any nation will not listen, then I will completely uproot it and destroy it, says the Lord. (Jer 12:17)
- Then pay attention to how you listen; for to those who have, more will be given; and from those who do not have, even what they seem to have will be taken away. (Luke 8:18)

Listening Rewarded

- If you will listen to all that I command you, walk in my ways, and do what is right in my sight by keeping my statutes and my commandments, as David my servant did, I will be with you, and will build you an enduring house. (1 Kgs 11:38)
- But it is for you, O Lord, that I wait; it is you, O Lord my God, who will answer. (Ps 38:15)
- Listen to advice and accept instruction, that you may gain wisdom for the future. (Prov 19:20)

CHAPTER 10
Decision-Making

Where two or more are gathered for collaboration or team-work, decision-making will inevitably happen among them. Understanding how and when decision-making works is a smart way to prevent collaborative efforts from breaking down or collapsing entirely. You'll also want to invest time and effort in learning if and when generational differences might have an impact on the decision-making process. Onward!

Point of Clarification: Teamwork and Collaboration

Clarifying from the get-go whether you're aiming for team-work or collaboration reduces at least one potential source of confusion.

- *Teamwork:* Two or more people share information and resources to achieve shared goals (i.e., what to accomplish). *Leadership:* One person appointed or elected. *Duration:* Disbanded after goal is achieved.

- *Collaboration:* Two or more people share goals, information, and resources to create something new to support shared purpose (i.e., reason to seek those goals). *Leadership:* Emerges as needed. *Duration:* Ongoing as needed.

Note: Cooperation involves exchanging information and resources to achieve individual goals. Cooperation, teamwork, and collaboration can all be undermined by manipulation (e.g., distorting or withholding information, rumor-mongering). Members of teams or collaborative efforts are also susceptible to cooptation (i.e., being given a role to lull them into going along with a leader's agenda).

You won't have to log much mileage on a church council or committees to generate a list of barriers that typically undermine decision-making in some parish environments. Decision-making (and true collaboration) is extraordinarily difficult in churches structured as rigidly hierarchical bureaucracies and where clerical authority is confused with leadership.[1]

Ironically, decision-making can also be stalled in churches where members declare that God is in control to obscure their derelictions of corporate action.[2]

But even if everyone involved is gung-ho about group process, decision-making can get bogged down for any number of reasons. Topping that list is when participants confuse consensus with agreement. Under the best of circumstances, leaders will make every effort to clarify how consensus does not require agreement for a decision to stand (see appendix B: Decision-Making 101). Congrats to anyone feeling safe enough to emphasize the perils of conformity. Extra points if "consensual validation" also gets explained.[3]

It's Consensus If You . . .

- receive the information and resources you need to make a decision;
- listen to others and are able to raise questions and concerns;
- get your questions and concerns addressed in a direct and clear way;

- understand that consensus is not the same as unanimity; and then
- agree with the proposed action *or* agree to set aside disagreements for the sake of reaching consensus.

It's Conformity If You. . .

- receive the information and resources you need to make a decision;
- listen to others without raising questions and concerns;
- opt out of getting your questions and concerns addressed because you figure they are right and/or you don't have the energy or skills to make your case;
- believe unanimity is essential for consensus; and then
- go along with the proposed action because you want to fit in.

Include spiritual maturity on your list of barriers to decision-making in the world of church. It takes some degree of spiritual maturity to understand when process is more important than outcome. It takes a heaping big helping of spiritual maturity to remain physically and emotionally present when a decision-making process challenges belief and shakes up faith, or perhaps the religious structure for it. Instead of storming out of the room and quitting church council (physically *or* emotionally), a spiritually mature person will ask, "What is being revealed?" "Why am I getting so irked?" Okay, maybe not instead of storming out or quitting but maybe a month after doing that? I mention this for a friend.

Now add "strength of community" and "sense of belonging" to your list of impediments to decision-making. As I emphasized earlier, vigorously asserting community doesn't make it so (re-read chapter 7: Belonging).[4] Plenty of churches have members who attend worship without sharing a vision for the life of that parish. Not everyone who feels alienated or disaffected by their church (or denomination) leaves it. Some will stay despite their weakening sense of community. Some will not only stay but serve in leadership if they're appointed or elected, doing so for reasons that have nothing to do with ego gratification. News flash: this is true for clergy and religious as well as laity.

Finally for here and now, make sure "trust" is on your list of impediments to decision-making. Unlike grace freely given, trust must be earned. You can count on trust issues flaring up when adults of all ages collaborate. Much of that mutual apprehension can be resolved by identifying, acknowledging, and discussing whatever might be swirling below the surface. Because it involves communication, decision-making does seem to be an area of engagement where paying attention to generationally specific attitudes and behaviors makes sense.

All Hail the Teachable Moment

There's a term for that special time when situations, participants' attitudes (or vulnerabilities), and timing align enough for significant learning to happen: the teachable moment.[5]

Teachable moments cannot be planned, they're situational. We can, however, add this to our conceptual toolkit and notice when teachable moments emerge. Since collaboration is an ongoing process, count on encountering at least one as you work with adults older and younger than you.

For example, we now have enough data to make valid generalizations about how each generational cohort approaches work, leadership, and authority.[6] Knowing about these documented differences in style will make it easier to address whatever might undermine decision-making. Please take a few minutes to study the chart for clues about the optimal mix of generations for team projects, and notice what you might need to accommodate for effective collaboration among adults.

Generations at Work					
	Silent Generation	**Boomers**	**Generation X**	**Millennials**	**Generation Z**
Work Ethos	Individualistic Work Hard Follow Rules	Competitive Workaholic Seek Efficiency	Self-Reliant Entrepreneurial Want Direction	Confident Ambitious Goal-Oriented	Self-directed Entrepreneurial Resourceful
Leadership Style	Firm Directive Hierarchical	Consensus	Competence-Based Inquiry-Driven	Collaborative	Collaborative
Attitude Toward Authority	Respectful	Questioning	Unimpressed	Polite	Distrustful

Some pain points such as clashing vocabularies of meaning and generationally specific jargon abuse are relatively simple to soothe. Just ask for clarification without sounding snotty. Full disclosure: I fail miserably at this. I seem unable to ask what, exactly, "church planting," "missional," "witness," and even "preaching the Gospel" means without sounding snotty.

Speaking of disclosure—younger and older adults seem to have difficulty recognizing and respecting generational differences in self-disclosure, self-expression, and definitions of psychological safety.

Like it or not, one generation's TMI (Too Much Information) is another's transparency (translation: honesty). GenXers and Millennials tend to share feelings, thoughts, and perceptions that some older Boomers and members of the Silent Generation consider cringe-worthy. It's also true that GenXers and Millennials have been seen to wince when older Boomers and members of the Silent Generation share their experience in the form of advice. "When I was your age, we. . . ."

Understand it or not, Millennials are acutely aware of what psychological safety looks, sounds, and feels like but not necessarily because they're "narcissistic."[7] Remember that this is the generation whose cultural defining moments have included international terrorism on domestic soil, domestic terrorism, and mass shootings at schools and universities. Failing to address their psychological reality only fuels their reluctance to participate in collaborative processes.

Many of these personal safety situations call for love-thy-neighbor attention and sympathy if empathy is not immediately possible. Although it was developed as a psychotherapeutic tactic, practicing "unconditional positive regard" will also help healing for everyone involved. In case you don't already know and a reminder if you do, unconditional positive regard is a commitment to accept and love people for who and where they are by treating them with consideration and respect.[8]

Meanwhile, it's impossible to envision, decide, and plan without differences of opinion, so in addition to paying attention to how "feedback" is delivered, clarifying the difference between criticism and critique benefits everyone.[9]

Point of Clarification:
Criticism and Critique

Wherever there are people, there will be opinions, some of which will be delivered and received badly. Knowing the difference between criticism and critique will help you provide useful and supportive feedback.

Criticism: Judgmental, vague, fault-finding, and negative evaluation. Delivery is usually opinionated and humorless. Negative criticism often reveals the insecurities, jealousies, and fears of whoever delivers it. Typical result: recipients feel attacked and defensive; critics feel frustrated and annoyed; everyone feels devitalized and stays stuck in place.

Critique: Nonjudgmental, specific, clarity-seeking, and helpful evaluation. Delivery is usually objective and good-humored. Rigorous critique often reveals the skills, experiences, and passions of whoever delivers it. Typical result: recipients feel supported and encouraged to grow; critics feel useful and valuable; everyone feels energized and motivated to move forward.

While it's tempting to focus on younger adults because they've been vocal about things like trigger warnings, they're not the only ones feeling uncomfortably at risk.[10] Adults of all ages opt out of church participation because they don't feel safe enough to "speak truth to power."[11] Church leadership tends not to realize this because older adults are less likely to openly raise such issues. They don't feel safe enough to say they don't feel safe. In the context of decision-making this includes not feeling safe to disagree, debate, argue, or share anything that might generate real or imagined conflict.

What to do?

Commit to getting and staying open, honest, and clear about rules and expectations for decision-making:

- Learn more about decision-making process options, and then choose one that will work in alignment with your congregation's culture. Note: your local church's culture may differ in some ways from the dominant culture of your denomination.

- Clarify group norms for interaction as well as consequences of violating them. Note: reluctance or complete failure to enforce consequences isn't being a good Christian, it's disrespecting the group.

- Create a clear protocol for hearing complaints that protects confidentiality but does not allow anonymity. Note: do not sacrifice rigor for speed, but don't drag out due process with the eternal hope it will all work out because God is in control.

- Adopt or adapt a clear process for dealing with conflict. Note: your church may already have an established conflict resolution process but don't let that stop you from studying others that are structured to reduce reactivity (e.g., principled negotiation; conflict transformation).[12]

**Principled Negotiation according to
Roger Fisher and William Ury**

Principled negotiation is a methodology for
dealing with differences and disputes based on
the assumption that positional bargaining is counterproductive. It
was developed during the late 1970s at the Harvard Negotiation
Project cofounded by Roger Fisher (1922–2012) and William
Ury (1953–). Fisher and Ury counsel being "hard on the merits,
soft on the people" using these four main principles:[13]

Principle I: Separate the People from the Problem
Because people are involved, disconnects in perceptions, emotions, and communications are predictable. Principled negotiation involves revealing and exploring these disconnects.

Principle II: Focus on Interests, Not Positions
Positions are based on interests, which may be in compe-
tition if not complete opposition. Principled negotiation
involves revealing and exploring these interests.

Principle III: Invent Options for Mutual Gain
Options (or solutions) are usually limited by assumptions
about what's desirable and possible. Principled negotiation
separates creating options from choosing among them.

Principle IV: Insist on Objective Criteria
In a contest of wills, one person will have to back down.
Principled negotiation involves jointly developing objective
criteria for what parties agree is fair.

As is the case with everything else within and beyond congregations, decision-making is an opportunity for adults to cultivate common ground for shared values to take root and flourish.
Deciding to engage in effective decision-making is a good way
to begin. Just saying.

Your Reality Check-Up:
Decision-Making

Contemplate your current reality and move forward by discussing:

- When am I most likely to participate in decision-making processes?

- Which part of this chapter generated the most anxiety for me? What might be the source of that anxiety?

- Which decision-making skills do I need to develop, enhance, or resurrect?

Let's Get Biblical—Decision-Making

Decision-Making Guidelines
- Choose for each of your tribes individuals who are wise, discerning, and reputable to be your leaders. (Deut 1:13)
- Let us choose what is right; let us determine among us ourselves what is good. (Job 34:4)
- Be still before the Lord, and wait patiently. (Ps 37:7)
- Fools think their own way is right, but the wise listen to advice. (Prov 12:15)
- Without counsel, plans go wrong, but with many advisers they succeed. (Prov 15:22)
- Now during those days [Jesus] went out to the mountain to pray; and he spent the night in prayer to God. (Luke 6:12)
- If any of you is lacking in wisdom, ask God, who gives to all generously and grudgingly, and it will be given you. (Jas 1:5)

- Whatever you do, do everything for the glory of God. (1 Cor 10:31)

Guidance Sought
- Teach me, and I will be silent; make me understand how I have gone wrong. (Job 6:24)
- Search me, O God, and know my heart; test me and know my thoughts. See if there is any wicked way in me, and lead me in the way everlasting. (Ps 139:23-24)
- Teach me to do your will, for you are my God. Let your good spirit lead me on a level path. (Ps 143:10)

Guidance Delivered
- I have set before you life and death, blessings and curses. Choose life so that you and your descendants may live. (Deut 30:19)
- Now if you are unwilling to serve the Lord, choose this day whom you will serve. . . . But as for me and my household, we will serve the Lord. (Josh 24:15)
- The precepts of the Lord are right, rejoicing the heart; the commandment of the Lord is clear, enlightening the eyes. (Ps 19:8)
- Who are they that fear the Lord? He will teach them the way that they should choose. (Ps 25:12)
- Trust in the Lord with all your heart, and do not rely on your own insight. (Prov 3:5)

CHAPTER 11
Embracing Change

Change? No, thank you. It's too challenging and scary, although we grudgingly accept changes in work and family life. But at church? Not so much. We expect comfort and consolation in the familiar predictability of it all. Gird your whatevers for this understatement: embracing change at church is difficult and often upsetting.

One glorious Sunday you arrive for worship to discover every pew has been removed so that seating can be flexibly configured. Or the crying room has been closed down permanently because babies belong to Beloved Community. Or the printed newsletter that you, for one, always toss into recycling without reading is now available only online. How. Dare. They.

Okay, so maybe it was time for a change. The pews were an ecological barrier to listening and obstacles for people in wheelchairs and walkers (see chapter 9: Listening). In addition to becoming a deterrent to participation, the crying room sucked up much-needed gathering space. A congregational survey revealed that you weren't the only one ignoring printed materials. But why did these changes have to happen so quickly? Whose ideas were these anyway? Gee, maybe that's what those congregational listening sessions were about?

God Never Changes

Hate change in general? Really hate change at church? You probably want to memorize this prayer attributed to St. Teresa of Ávila. It's commonly known as St. Teresa's Bookmark because after her death in 1582, it was found tucked into her prayer book.[1] Search and you'll find different translations of this prayer:

Let nothing disturb you;
let nothing frighten you.
All things are passing.
God never changes.
Patience obtains all things.
Nothing is wanting to those who possess God.
God alone suffices.

Some percentage of congregational change has been simmering on a back burner for years. Something or someone turns up the heat and a change process begins officially. Sometimes a crisis requires swift parish-level change without much of a public collaborative process. In either case, change agents typically emerge from among longtime congregants; some of them in leadership, but not necessarily. Other change agents are newcomers. (Spoiler Alert: These aren't always younger adults. Plenty of middle-age and older adults switch congregations.) New congregants bring fresh perspectives, first noticing and then pointing out how:

- worship times don't accommodate young families or older adults;

- worship attendance could be boosted by offering a live-streaming option;

- committee participation, especially for anything scheduled at night would benefit from using an online meeting platform;

- registration for events would be more efficiently accomplished online;
- leadership has been in place for so long it no longer reflects the congregation's diversity; and/or
- decision-making would be enhanced by a simplified process.

Sometimes newcomers go beyond pointing stuff out and enthusiastically offer to implement change. But, oh dear Lord, it's *change* and they're *newcomers*. How. Dare. They.[2]

Change may happen so slowly and incrementally that it barely registers on your personal radar screen. Eventually you get around to noticing ushers and church council members wearing nametags during Sunday worship. Other changes seem radical because they've come down (or been imposed) from higher levels of church without being fully communicated. You're stunned to realize that judicatory-level leadership changed not only the structures but labels for church ministries and the ministers therein.

When changes make sense, you go along with them. If the impetus for change isn't obvious, you might ask why it happened—and then become a change agent to change the change. After all, one person's "moving forward" is another person's "moving backward." Especially in church.[3]

Change is so anxiety-provoking that even the most intentionally inclusive congregations can be disrupted by emotions and less-than-helpful behaviors that flare up when change is proposed. Of course there are always a few congregants who will quickly reframe their change-related tension as excitement. Those people are usually more interested in complete transformation than they are mere change. Despite faith professed and the ability to quote Pierre Teilhard de Chardin about trusting the "slow work of God," everyone else will seem pretty much gripped by fear.[4] And that fear will eventually manifest as resistance, but I'll get to that. First, more about fears that emerge when the inevitability of change starts sinking in.[5]

You Want Change If You . . .

- want to improve what already exists;
- tinker with past constraints;
- have a replacement mindset;
- modify actions; and/or
- create something that can be reversed or reverted.

You Want Transformation If You . . .

- want to create something new;
- release past constraints;
- have a radical mindset;
- modify values; and/or
- create something that generates forward movement.

Thanks to psychologists, we know a lot about fear in general. Fears can either be traced to experience or are irrational. Fears can prevent growth or provide effective emotional shelter from harm. Identifying fears is a necessary step toward facing them.

Thanks to experts in managing organizational change, we know a lot about fear during that institutional-level change process. Fears are normal and predictable when organizations change. Acknowledging and addressing change-related fears is necessary for mitigating resistance to organizational change. When we categorize change-related fears by the core issues adults share, they map out like this:

Identity-related Fears
include but are not limited to fear of:

- not being respected;
- no longer knowing status and role in community; and

- being unable to change.

Purpose-related Fears
include but are not limited to fear of:

- the unknown future;
- a predictable and disliked future; and
- being discarded or replaced.

Belonging-related Fears
include but are not limited to fear of:

- not being listened to or heard;
- relationships changing; and
- no longer fitting in.

Legacy-based Fears
include but are not limited to fear of:

- losing history and culture;
- being left out or left behind; and
- being forgotten.

Like the core issues shared by adults, these basic fears are not experienced exclusively by any particular generation. Don't bother trying to predict which generation is most likely to become apathetic, exhausted, cynical, discouraged, frustrated, hostile, negative, or skeptical about change in church. For every young adult who says/tweets/posts that something "will never happen," there's a middle-aged adult thinking, "That never turns out well." Meanwhile, older adults are muttering about being dead before change happens or dropping dead because it has.

> ### Managing Transitions according to William Bridges
>
> During the late 1970s, William Bridges (1933–2013) brought a generation to awareness about transition as an essential part of the change process for individuals as well as organizations. Bridges' three-stage model for the slow process of transition remains meaningful for adults of all ages.[6]
>
> #### *The Bridges Transitions Model*
>
> Stage I: Endings
> > Something ends. Feelings of anger, shock, frustration, loss, grief, and confusion are predictable even when the ending is planned or anticipated. Internal process involves: separating and getting closure (a.k.a. letting go).
>
> Stage II: Neutral Zone
> > Time and space between ending and beginning something new. Feelings of chaos, discomfort, discouragement, skepticism, and uncertainty. Internal process involves: acknowledging and managing waiting.
>
> Stage III: New Beginnings
> > Something new is fully accepted (vs. started). Feelings of hope, enthusiasm, anxiety, and impatience. Internal process involves: balancing paradoxical feelings and emotions.

As I've pointed out elsewhere, fears are feelings with multiple layers.[7] Here and now, I want to highlight how grief often lurks beneath fear of change.

Because this grief can almost always be traced to feeling the loss of "what it was like," I believe it's better interpreted as expressed nostalgia. By way of contrast, announcing "We've always done it this way" is more accurately viewed as hostility.[8] And nostalgia? Not a bad thing and should not automatically be dismissed as "euphoric recall." According to psychologists who study it, nostalgia tends to boost generosity and tolerance, especially toward outsiders.[9]

Fear predictably leads to resistance, another thing that change management theorists and practitioners have identified in detail. How does resistance show up? Oh, you know—the usual human stuff like obstruction and opposition in its many annoying forms. The short list of passively aggressive maneuvers includes things like forgetting to read materials, missing meetings, not responding to email or text messages. The short list of blatantly aggressive maneuvers includes consciously deciding to not send out materials or let members know about meetings; shouting others down, if not during a meeting then in the church parking lot afterward.

Wait, what? These things happen among people of faith? Yes, yes they do. Neither church attendance nor participation makes us divine. We always remain fully human. Our Christian faith can rescue us, but two things need to be solidly in place: (1) a rigorous process for calling out bad behavior without spiritualizing it away and (2) mechanisms for accountability that don't threaten loss of salvation or eternal life! I'm only partly kidding about how to construct mechanisms for accountability. Only you can say whether your church flogs troublesome (or troublemaking) members with the sin whip.

Tempting as it may be to avoid seeing, naming, and dealing with resistance, change will not happen without doing all that. In fact, I feel quite comfy asserting that change will be more readily embraced if resistance is met with forthright clarity and compassion. Opposition and obstruction by individuals and entire disaffected groups within any congregation can be significantly reduced by addressing questions about the:

- *Need for change:* How have we identified key issues? How often have the same or similar concerns been raised? For how long have these issues been raised? How many congregants are negatively affected by the status quo? How will we engage with congregants who truly believe everything is fine? Which is greater, the risks of changing or not changing? How will we learn more about why other congregations made similar changes?

- *Change process:* Who will participate in the change process? How will we select representatives from interest groups? Do we want to establish a quota system to ensure participation? How will we deal with representative groups opting-out of participating? Which decision-making process will we use? How swiftly or slowly do we want to change? How swiftly or slowly do we need to change? How will we announce changes? What support will we offer to help everyone deal with the emotional realities of transitioning? Are we willing and able to deal with those who obstruct and undermine change? How will we learn more about changes used successfully by other congregations?[10]

- *Timetable for change:* How much time should elapse between deciding what needs to change and making that change? How will we schedule and pace changes? How will we roll out changes? How will we honor our past while celebrating changes?

Reducing Resistance to Change according to John P. Kotter and Leonard A. Schlesinger

Among the notable contributions to understanding organizational change, the work of John P. Kotter (1947–) and Leonard A. Schlesinger (1953–) has stood the test of time and changes in culture. Their six strategies for reducing resistance are based on recognizing what gets in the way: self-interest, misunderstanding, low tolerance for change, and disagreements about the need for change.[11]

Kotter and Schlesinger's Six Approaches for Dealing with Resistance to Change

Education and Communication

> *Source of Resistance:* Information is unclear, inaccurate, or insufficient.
> *Tactics:* Go beyond informing to educating about why change is needed and the expected implementation.
> *Downside:* lack of clarity in communication

Participation and Involvement

> *Source of Resistance:* Initiators don't seem to be listening to those who will be affected, especially those with power to thwart change.
> *Tactics:* Create forums and processes for listening to questions and concerns.
> *Downside:* time-consuming

Facilitation and Support

> *Source of Resistance:* anxiety, fear, and other negative emotional responses by those who will be affected
> *Tactics:* Provide training as well as emotional support.
> *Downside:* time-consuming and expensive

Negotiation and Agreement

> *Source of Resistance:* those affected who will lose something and have the power to resist

> *Tactics:* negotiated agreements
> *Downside:* expensive
>
> Manipulation and Cooptation
> *Tactics:* Provide selective information and consciously
> structure events.
> *Downside:* emotionally dishonest
>
> Explicit and Implicit Coercion
> *Tactics:* Force change with explicit or implicit threats.
> *Downside:* mean-spirited and disrespectful

As a practical matter, make every effort to ensure that unstated questions get articulated and asked. Discussing fears and concerns proactively rather than reactively always ends up being the path to much less resistance.

I love the well-worn one-liner about change in the church: "We're the church; we'll get back to you in 500 years." Not so off-base when you take the long view of Christian church history. But because we worship and live out our faith at the local church level, most of us will encounter congregational change and more than once. Not too keen about change? Go find other congregants who are. Don't be at all surprised if they're older or younger than you.

Your Reality Check-Up: Change

Contemplate your current reality and move forward by discussing:

• What do I treasure most about "the way we've always done it"?

• When do I most long for and am willing to become a change agent?

• Who in my church community is most likely to embrace change?

Let's Get Biblical—Change

God Never Changes

• Give thanks to the Lord, for he is good; for his steadfast love endures forever. (1 Chr 16:34)

• But you, O Lord, are enthroned forever; your name endures to all generations. (Ps 102:12)

• Your kingdom is an everlasting kingdom, and your dominion endures throughout all generations. The Lord is faithful in all his words, and gracious in all his deeds. (Ps 145:13)

• Trust in the Lord forever, for in the Lord God you have an everlasting rock. (Isa 26:4)

• I know that whatever God does endures forever; nothing can be added to it, nor anything taken from it; God has done this, so that all should stand in awe before him. (Eccl 3:14)

• For I the Lord do not change; therefore you, O children of Jacob, have not perished. (Mal 3:6)

Everything Else Changes

- For everything there is a season, and a time for every matter under heaven. (Eccl 3:1)
- Listen, I will tell you a mystery! We will not all die, but we will all be changed. (1 Cor 15:51)
- So if anyone is in Christ, there is a new creation: everything old has passed away; see, everything is become new! (2 Cor 5:17)
- There is no longer Jew or Greek, there is no longer slave or free, there is no longer male and female; for all of you are one in Christ Jesus. (Gal 3:28)

APPENDIX A
Listening 101

What's that? You've already encountered these tips for listening? Since they were probably embedded in an omnibus list of communication skills, here they are again. To listen more effectively:

- *Become willing.* Starting from a baseline of "don't want to hear it" undermines listening. While you're at it, suspend judgment to get beyond hearing and into listening.

- *Stop talking.* With the possible exception of the highly specialized skill of simultaneous translation, listening and speaking cannot happen at the same time. You'll need to shut up.[1]

- *Cultivate patience.* Plan to encounter people who do not speak as clearly, swiftly, or logically as (you believe) you speak. Cultivating patience in advance is easier than generating it in real time.

- *Pay attention to speakers' verbal and nonverbal clues.* Notice the order in which information is presented, parenthetical comments and quips, word choices, and voice tone as well as body posture, facial expressions, and eye movements. These signs and signals reveal messages that speakers may not realize they're conveying.

- *Provide nonverbal cues for speakers.* Periodically smile and nod your head to assure speakers that you're listening. Monitor your own body posture and facial expressions for signifiers of boredom and incredulity (e.g., frowning, eye rolling).[2] Make direct eye contact without staring, glaring, or glazing over. Doing this will enhance your ability to listen even if you're part of a large audience.[3]

- *Learn to listen with ease.* Pitching forward, developing a headache, struggling to focus, and feeling confused are signs of listening too hard. Take a deep breath and relax, or ask for a brief time-out.

- *Seek clarification.* Questions like, "Did I hear you say . . . ?" or "Am I correct in thinking . . . ?" let speakers know you're listening. Periodically summarize what you think you've heard to get a reality check for your listening. These "active listening" techniques are also nonaggressive ways to check assumptions and correct misperceptions. Caution: Watch out for coming across as pseudo-therapeutic or patronizing.

- *Don't interrupt.* Let others finish their thoughts even if they blather on. Not only is interrupting rude, it's counterproductive because most people will start over their spiel from the beginning.[4]

- *Keep listening.* Don't stop listening when you hear something that seems odd, wrong, unfair, or bad. Keep listening to glean insights into what might really be going on, then seek clarification.

APPENDIX B
Decision-Making 101

Given the difficulty most people have making their own decisions, no one should be surprised that group decision-making can become convoluted. Conflicts inevitably emerge because of differences in temperament, personality, and communication style. Disparities in authority, power, and influence also have an impact on decision-making processes.

Choosing and using time-tested structures and processes for decision-making will help optimize conditions for collaboration whether or not a decision has to be made. Reminding everyone that Jesus the Christ is present wherever two or three are gathered in his name is wise, as is beginning and ending meetings with prayer.

Participation

How will people engage with the issues and one another? How and when will disagreements be discussed? How will idiosyncratic or downright iconoclastic ideas been received and managed? How and when may participants ask for clarification? ProTip: Processes improve exponentially when the facilitator has formal training.[1] Options to consider:

- structured debate
- round-robin discussion

- limits on the number of times any one person may contribute

- mechanisms to reduce repeating points/proposals

- limits on the amount of time for presentations/discussions

Voting

How will decisions be made? May members abstain? When should one voting process shift to another (e.g., from voice vote to written ballot)? Who will be authorized to tally votes? Options to consider:

Timing for Voting
- after a predetermined period of time for discussion has ended
- when the group agrees a discussion is finished or finished enough
- when anyone calls for a vote (i.e., "calling the question")
- when a true "Sense of the Meeting" emerges[2]

Manner of Voting
- ballot
- raised hands
- voice

Decision Rules

Who or what determines if a decision will stand? Options to consider:

- simple majority

- super-majority (i.e., at least two-thirds or other predetermined threshold)

- consensus (i.e., individuals set aside any unresolved concerns and agree to support a decision for the good of the group)[3]

- unanimous consent/general agreement (i.e., all group members agree)[4]

- leadership decides

Refreshments

How will body and mind be physically supported, especially during a long and possibly contentious deliberative process? How will health/medical conditions be accommodated? ProTips:

- Water is a must-have, either tap or bottled.

- Other Beverages:
  - caffeinated and noncaffeinated
  - sugar and sugar-free
  - no alcohol before or during (include alcohol-free options after)

- Snacks:
  - gluten-free options
  - high-protein options
  - dairy-free options
  - fresh fruit options

Notes

Preface

1. For a Storify transcript of this chat, visit: http://bit.ly/1NF8Zgf.

Chapter 1: About Age and Aging

1. For more about prefrontal cortex development and its impact on behavior, see Jay N. Giedd, "The Teen Brain: Insights from Neuroimaging," *Journal of Adolescent Health* 42, no. 4 (2008): 335–43, http://bit.ly/2elMnu4; Sara B. Johnson, Robert W. Blum, and Jay N. Giedd, "Adolescent Maturity and the Brain: The Promise and Pitfalls of Neuroscience Research in Adolescent Health Policy," *Journal of Adolescent Health* 45, no. 3 (2009): 216–21, http://bit.ly/2elMJRF.

2. Nine vaccine-preventable diseases, including smallpox, polio, cholera, and typhoid, were basically eliminated by the mid-twentieth century. See CDC National Immunization Program, "Achievements in Public Health, 1900–1999 Impact of Vaccines Universally Recommended for Children— United States, 1990–1998," *Morbidity and Mortality Weekly Report*, April 2, 1999, http://bit.ly/2bqalFf. Alas, we currently have the "anti-vaxxers" to thank for a resurgence of death by measles. Arguing with them is an exercise in futility: Laura June, "Twitter Study Finds Facts Don't Matter to Anti-Vaxxers," *The Cut*, April 12, 2016, http://thecut.io/2bqa5pZ.

3. Elizabeth Fain and Cara Weatherford, "Comparative Study of Millennials' (age 20–34 years) Grip and Lateral Pinch with the Norms," *Journal of Hand Therapy* 29, no. 4 (2016), http://bit.ly/2bZxvgW. For the fun version, read Natalie Jacewicz, "Millennials May Be Losing Their Grip," *Shots* (blog), *NPR*, June 13, 2016, http://n.pr/2bZvNfN.

4. White men born in 1935 were expected to live to age 60; white women to age 64; black men to age 51; black women to age 55. The retirement age

was sixty-five. By 2014, life expectancy at birth increased more for blacks than for whites; also slightly increased for Hispanic females and males. See National Center for Health Statistics, *Health, United States, 2015: With Special Feature on Racial and Ethnic Health Disparities* (Hyattsville, MD: National Center for Health Statistics, 2016), 20: "Race is a social construct influenced by a complex set of factors. Because of the complexity and difficulty in conceptualizing and defining race, as well as the increasing representation of racial and ethnic subgroups in the United States, racial classification and data collection systems continue to evolve and expand."

5. These distinctions first showed up in: D. E. Forman, A. D. Berman, C. H. McCabe, D. S. Baim, and J. Y. Wei, "PTCA in the Elderly: The 'Young-old' versus the 'Old-old,'" *Journal of American Geriatric Society* 40, no. 1 (1992): 19–22, http://1.usa.gov/1XNdVtl; C. A. Zizza, K. J. Ellison, and C. M. Wernette, "Total Water Intakes of Community-Living Middle-Old and Oldest-Old Adults," *The Journals of Gerontology Series A: Biological Sciences and Medical Sciences* 64, no. 4 (2009): 481–86, http://1.usa.gov/24HdFKI; "The Demographics of Our Aging Population," Transgenerational Design Matters, http://www.transgenerational.org/aging/demographics.htm.

6. Social historians offer another perspective about how age is perceived. See, for example: Howard P. Chudacoff, *How Old Are You? Age Consciousness in American Culture* (Princeton, NJ: Princeton University Press, 1989). See also Philippe Ariès, *Centuries of Childhood: A Social History of Family Life* (New York: Vintage, 1965). Despite being considered a major contribution to the field of family history, a small industry emerged among scholars who focused on proving Ariès wrong. For an overview of that academic ker-fuffle, see Anastasia Ulanowicz, "Philippe Ariès," Representing Childhood, Center for Instructional Development & Distance Education (CIDDE), University of Pittsburgh, http://bit.ly/29MI1v4 [PDF].

7. Early-onset (a.k.a., younger onset) Alzheimer's is defined as such when it occurs in anyone younger than age 65. While people as young as age 30 have been diagnosed with early-onset Alzheimer's, this occurs in less than 10 percent of all people with Alzheimer's and is generally due to an inherited gene. For more information, see Alzheimer's Disease Education and Referral Center, "Alzheimer's Disease Fact Sheet," *National Institute on Aging*, http://bit.ly/2nBRIz7.

Chapter 2: Exploring Psychosocial Development

1. For a six-stage theory of lifecycle development based on growing consciousness and letting go of childhood myths, see Roger L. Gould, *Transformations: Growth and Change in Adult Life* (New York: Simon & Schuster, 1979). For a description of the human lifecycle in twelve stages, see Thomas Armstrong, *The Human Odyssey: Navigating the Twelve Stages of Life* (New York: Sterling, 2008). For an eight-stage "eco-soulcentric" approach that provides archetypes like the "soul apprentice at the well-spring" (a.k.a. early adulthood), see Bill Plotkin, *Nature and the Human Soul: Cultivating Wholeness and Community in a Fragmented World* (Novato, CA: New World Library, 2007).

2. The term "adolescence" was first coined by psychologist G. Stanley Hall, who published *Adolescence: Its Psychology and Its Relation to Physiology, Anthropology, Sociology, Sex, Crime, Religion and Education* in 1904.

3. Ken Dychtwald and Joe Flower, *Age Wave: How the Most Important Trend of Our Time Will Change Your Future* (New York: Bantam, 1990); Sara Lawrence-Lightfoot, *The Third Chapter: Passion, Risk and Adventure in the 25 Years after 50* (New York: Sara Crichton, 2009); Zalman Schacter-Shalomi and Ronald S. Miller, *From Age-ing to Sage-ing* (New York: Warner, 1999).

4. The following is adapted from Eric H. Erikson, *The Lifecycle Completed: A Review* (New York: W. W. Norton, 1982).

5. Begin reading about this debate with Jeffrey Jensen Arnett, "Emerging Adulthood: A Theory of Development from the Late Teens through the 20s," *American Psychologist* 55, no. 5 (2000): 469–80, http://bit.ly/29Gan7i. Follow that up with the popular book by Kelly Williams Brown, *Adulting: How to Become a Grown-up in 468 Easy(ish) Steps* (New York: Grand Central, 2013). Alternatively, for a long but readable review of all of this conversation go directly to this article by Julie Beck, "When Are You Really an Adult?" *The Atlantic*, January 5, 2016, http://theatln.tc/29GbvIh. Beck cites Cheryl Merser, *"Grown-Ups": A Generation in Search of Adulthood* (New York: G. P. Putnam, 1987), a book I urge you to read because it's positively prophetic.

6. Yes, I know, it's a bit more complex than that, but I'm sparing you a complete review of the introductory psychology course you took during undergraduate school. You did take Psychology 101, right? Also, Sociology 101, Introduction to Cultural Anthropology, Economics 101, and Political Science 101, yes? If not, you have my generation to thank for obliterating the core curriculum. We were so wrong.

7. In my (almost never) humble opinion, Levinson should have received an award for stating, "It is essential to keep in mind that development is not synonymous with growth." See Daniel J. Levinson, "A Conception of Adult Development," *American Psychologist* 41, no. 1 (1986): 3–13.

8. The following is adapted from ibid.

9. For an excellent, readable book about what is—and isn't—new in the trajectory of human development, hunker down with Robin Marantz Henig and Samantha Henig, *Twentysomething: Why Do Young Adults Seem Stuck?* (New York: Hudson Street, 2012).

10. Who are these theorists? James W. Fowler rolled out his stages of faith in *Stages of Faith: The Psychology of Human Development and the Quest for Meaning* (San Francisco, CA: HarperSanFrancisco, 1981). During the late 1950s, Lawrence Kohlberg built his theory of moral development on the foundation established by Jean Piaget during the 1930s in the latter's *The Moral Judgment of the Child* (New York: Free Press, 1965). By the late 1970s, gender biases of Kohlberg's theory were challenged by Carol Gilligan, *In a Different Voice: Psychological Theory and Women's Development* (Boston, MA: Harvard University Press, 1982).

11. For a critique of the influence of developmental psychology, see Holly Catterton Allen and Christine Lawson, *Intergenerational Christian Formation: Bringing the Whole Church Together in Ministry, Community and Worship* (Downers Grove, IL: InterVarsity Press, 2012), 35–46. See also John Roberto, *Reimagining Faith Formation for the 21st Century: Engaging All Ages & Generations* (Naugatuck, CT: Lifelong Faith Associates, 2015).

Chapter 3: Understanding Generations

1. Useful resources about the impact of multiple generations within the same congregation, see: Edward H. Hammett with Paul L. Anderson and Cornell Thomas, *Reaching People under 30, While Keeping People Over 60: Creating Community Across Generations* (Danvers, MA: TCP, 2015) and Gary L. McIntosh, *One Church, Four Generations: Understanding and Reaching All Ages in Your Church* (Grand Rapids, MI: Baker, 2002).

2. While not technically considered social scientists, marketers like Faith Popcorn and journalists like Gail Sheehy have made valuable contributions. Marketers usually get dissed for not being social scientific enough and having another agenda: sales. Journalists sometimes get dismissed because their work is readable.

3. Gail Sheehy, *New Passages: Mapping Your Life across Time* (New York: Ballantine, 1995).

4. The data here is from the Pew Research Center, which I consider the gold standard in this domain, in part because data analysis is more current than anything issued by the United States government. Note, however, that Sheehy, Howe, Strauss, and others in the field all define the ranges differently.

5. I'm leaving out the Greatest Generation (b. 1914–24) because most of them are no longer alive. The term was popularized by journalist Tom Brokaw in his book, *The Greatest Generation* (New York: Random House, 2001).

6. Reported as 55 percent Caucasian, 24 percent Hispanic, 14 percent African American, 4 percent Asian in Ruth Bernstein, "Move Over Millennials—Here Comes GenZ," in *AdvertisingAge,* January 21, 2015, http://bit.ly/2gOh89s.

7. "Generation Quiz: What Generation Am I?" *Are You There, God? It's Me, Generation X,* http://bit.ly/28WU1al; "How Millennial Are You?," *Pew Research Center,* http://pewrsr.ch/28WUxEZ; "How Millennial Are You?" *BrainFall,* http://bit.ly/28WUPvG. FWIW, I consistently test as Millennial, which might make me a Perennial and for more about that, see: Gina Pell, "Meet the Perennials," *theWhat* (blog), October 19, 2016, http://bit.ly/2g6dLMJ and Nancy Salamone, "Perennials—A Tale of Different Generations," Nancy Salamone: Capturing Your Share of the Women's Market, November 3, 2016, http://bit.ly/2g6cmG8.

8. Who comes up with these terms? Thanks for asking! For an overview, see Josh Sanburn, "How Every Generation of the Last Century Got Its Nickname," *Time,* December 1, 2015, http://ti.me/2hCgEU0. Here are a few key sources: For the World War II Generation, Vietnam Generation, and Me Generation, see Gail Sheehy, *New Passages: Mapping Your Life Across Time* (New York: Ballantine, 1995). For Thirteeners and Millennials, see Neil Howe and William Strauss, "The New Generation Gap," *The Atlantic,* December 1992, http://theatln.tc/2hBZPZy. For Generation X, see Doug Coupland, *Generation X: Tales for an Accelerated Culture* (New York: St. Martin's Press, 1991). For Generation Y, see Editorial, "Generation Y," *Advertising Age,* August 30, 1993, 16. For Builders, Busters, and Bridgers, see Gary L. McIntosh, *One Church, Four Generations: Understanding and Reaching All Ages in Your Church* (Grand Rapids, MI: Baker, 2002). For Peter Pan Generation and Boomerang Generation, see Kathleen Shaputis,

The Crowded Nest Syndrome: Surviving the Return of Adult Children (Olympia, WA: Clutter Fairy, 2004). For Echo Boomers, see Stephanie Armour, "Generation Y: They've Arrived at Work with a New Attitude," *USA Today*, November 6, 2008, http://usat.ly/2hCh5hd. For the Me Generation, see Jean Twenge, *Generation Me: Why Today's Young Americans are More Confident, Assertive, Entitled—and More Miserable than Ever Before*, updated ed. (New York: Atria, 2014).

9. As sociologist, journalist, and 1960s activist Todd Gitlin points out, "Generational blocs do not march like unified phalanxes." See Todd Gitlin, *Letters to a Young Activist* (New York: Basic, 2008), 30.

10. Significant intervening variable here: socioeconomic status (a.k.a. social class). As it turns out, racial minorities in the upper classes do tend to have more in common with whites in the upper classes than they do with racial minorities with low/no educational attainment and living in poverty. This reality makes a lot of social activists very uncomfortable.

11. For a blessedly readable description of cohort analysis that includes definitions and examples of life cycle/age, period, and cohort effect, see Pew Research Center, "The Whys and Hows of Generations Research," September 3, 2015, http://pewrsr.ch/28NuYca [pdf].

12. While it sounds like the term "generation gap" is something crafted during the late twentieth century, it emerged much earlier. For a dense but interesting (if you can plow through it) history of the term, see Gordon Welty, "The 'Generation Gap' Reconsidered," in *Global Youth, Peace, and Development: The Role of Science and Technology in Contemporary Society*, ed. Yedla C. Simadri, vol. 1 (Delhi: Ajanta, 1991), 383–99, http://bit.ly/2g6k7vS.

13. Michael S. North and Susan T. Fiske, "A prescriptive, intergenerational-tension ageism scale: Succession, Identity, and Consumption (SIC)," *Psychological Assessment* 25, no. 3 (2013): 706–13, http://bit.ly/2mAZf4q [pdf]; "Act your (old) age: Prescriptive, ageist biases over Succession, Consumption, and Identity," *Personality and Social Psychology Bulletin* 39, no. 6 (2013): 720–34, http://bit.ly/1UdhXUh [pdf].

14. For a delightfully snarktastic article challenging stereotypes about Millennials being entitled, lazy, apathetic, and technologically dependent, see Elizabeth Mount, "Here Is Why Millennials Are the Worst—and Why This Is Great News for Your Congregation," *Blue Boat* (blog), Unitarian Universalist Association, January 21, 2016, http://bit.ly/28WSqBc.

Chapter 4: A Bit about Stereotypes and Ageism

1. Anyone reading this *not* know I'm a sociologist? I only always mention my education and training when given the slightest opportunity.

2. The following is adapted from Henri Tajfel and John Turner, "An Integrative Theory of Intergroup Conflict," in *Psychology of Intergroup Relations*, ed. William G. Austin and Stephen Worchel (Chicago: Nelson-Hall, 1979), 33–47, http://bit.ly/2dUYL0K.

3. Socioeconomic status is sociological shorthand for a measure that combines education, occupation, and income. Non-sociologists refer to this as "social class."

4. During the 1970s through mid-1980s, much of my academic work focused on clarifying distinctions between sex and gender. Back then what seemed like difficult conceptual (and practical) challenges now seem so simple (and simplistic). In November 2016, digital dating app Tinder launched thirty-seven gender identity options; see Lucy Clarke-Billings, "What Do Tinder's 37 New Gender Identity Options Mean?," *Newsweek*, November 18, 2016, http://bit.ly/2gcNriO.

5. John Oliver Siy and Sapna Cheryan, "When Compliments Fail to Flatter: American Individualism and Responses to Positive Stereotypes," *Journal of Personality and Social Psychology* 104, no. 1 (2013): 87–102, http://bit.ly/1sBzGyu.

6. For a history of the psychological research about prejudice, see Scott Plous, "The Psychology of Prejudice, Stereotyping, and Discrimination: An Overview," in *Understanding Prejudice and Discrimination*, ed. Scott Plous (New York: McGraw-Hill, 2003), 3–48. For psychological impact of social exclusion, see C. Nathan DeWall, Timothy Deckman, Richard S. Pond Jr., and Ian Bonser, "Belongingness as a Core Personality Trait: How Social Exclusion Influences Social Functioning and Personality Expression," *Journal of Personality* 79, no. 6 (2001): 1281–314, http://bit.ly/2eo2uYs.

7. For the original interview, see Carl Bernstein, "Age and Race Fears Seen in Housing Opposition," *Washington Post*, March 7, 1969. See also R. N. Butler, "Age-Ism: Another Form of Bigotry," *The Gerontologist* 9, no. 4 (1969): 243–46.

8. For an overview of this research, see: Tina Adler, "Ageism: Alive and Kicking," *Observer* 26, no. 7 (2013), http://bit.ly/2dV2bRo.

Chapter 5: Identity

1. What about people diagnosed with Multiple Personality Disorder (MPD)? No longer an official thing. The diagnostic classification was changed to Dissociative Identity Disorder (DID) in 1994 to better describe difficulties with integrating aspects of identity and memory rather than multiple identities. For discussion, see Alexandria K. Cherry, "Multiple Personality Disorder: Fact or Fiction?," Great Ideas in Personality, http://bit.ly/2eplNR6. For more about controversies, see Robert Todd Carroll, "multiple personality disorder [dissociative identity disorder]," *The Skeptic's Dictionary*, http://bit.ly/2epnkqe.

2. Alexandra Robbins and Abby Wilner popularized the notion of a quarter-life crisis in their book, *Quarterlife Crisis: The Unique Challenges of Life in Your Twenties* (New York: J. P. Tarcher, 2001). For a stronger and more articulate case for the significance of young adulthood for identity development, read Meg Jay, *The Defining Decade: Why Your Twenties Matter—and How to Make the Most of Them Now* (New York: Twelve, 2012). Jay is also known for coming up with the notion of building "identity capital" by investing in self during young adulthood. Also watch her February 2013 TED talk, "Why 30 Is Not the New 20," *TED: Ideas Worth Spreading*, http://bit.ly/2dWdoRI. Another terrific, well-written read is Robin Marantz Henig and Samantha Henig, *Twenty Something: Why Do Young Adults Seem Stuck?* (New York: Hudson Street, 2012).

3. Motivational speakers love to claim that the Chinese symbol for crisis combines the characters for danger and opportunity. For decades they and others have used this to go on about growth opportunities available during times of crisis. While that spiritual principle about crisis and growth is true, claims about the Chinese ideogram are not. For more detailed information about how this "linguistic faux pas" is "due partly to wishful thinking," see Steve Nguyen, "In Chinese: Crisis Does Not Mean Danger and Opportunity," *Workplace Psychology* (blog), August 10, 2014, http://bit.ly/2h0usKI, which includes links to even more detailed analyses plus a citation to the John F. Kennedy quote from 1959 that allegedly started all the confusion. I'm especially enthralled by the detailed critique by Victor H. Mair, "danger + opportunity ≠ crisis: How a Misunderstanding about Chinese Characters Has Led Many Astray," Pīnyīn.info, http://bit.ly/2h0t7U1.

4. The following is adapted from James E. Marcia, "Development and Validation of Ego-Identity Status," *Journal of Personality and Social Psychology* 3,

no. 5 (1966): 551–58, http://bit.ly/2c8EPqV [pdf]. See also James E. Marcia, Alan S. Waterman, David R. Matteson, Sally L. Archer, Jacob L. Orlofsky, *Ego Identity: A Handbook for Psychosocial Research* (New York: Springer, 1993).

5. Chai there!

6. Erving Goffman, *Presentation of Self in Everyday Life* (New York: Anchor, 1959) is one of the classics that shaped the school of sociological theory known as symbolic interactionism. Great stuff to study in tandem with Donald Winnicott's work about true self and false self, as well as Carl Roger's work about congruent and incongruent self-concepts. If you need a project.

7. For more details about the religious aspects, see Committee on Divine Worship, "Fifteen Questions on the Quinceanera," United States Conference of Catholic Bishops, http://bit.ly/2c0nxMD.

Chapter 6: Purpose

1. Abraham H. Maslow, *Motivation and Personality*, 2nd ed. (New York: Harper & Row, 1970). Somewhat along the same lines, Carl Rogers (1902–87) pointed out how self-actualization cannot happen if there's a persistent disconnect among self-worth, self-image, and ideal self. See Carl Rogers, "A Theory of Therapy, Personality and Interpersonal Relationships as Developed in the Client-centered Framework," in *Formulations of the Person and the Social Context*, vol. 3 of *Psychology: A Study of a Science*, ed. Sigmund Koch (New York: McGraw-Hill, 1959).

2. Carl G. Jung identified these five basic factors "making for happiness in the human mind":

    1. Good physical and mental health.
    2. Good personal and intimate relationships, such as those of marriage, the family, and friendships.
    3. The faculty for perceiving beauty in art and nature.
    4. Reasonable standards of living and satisfactory work.
    5. A philosophic or religious point of voice capable of coping successfully with the vicissitudes of life.

He trotted these out during a 1960 interview with an English journalist. See Gordon Young, "The Art of Living: An Eighty-Fifth Birthday Interview for Switzerland," in *C. G. Jung Speaking: Interviews and Encounters*, ed. William McGuire and R. F. C. Hull, Bollingen Series (Princeton, NJ: Princeton University Press, 1977), 442–52, http://bit.ly/2cJf57m.

3. Whether you think life should be "meaningful," "fulfilling," or "purposeful" will depend on which decade you began paying attention to this

stuff. At this point in the twenty-first century, I wouldn't be surprised if someone writes a bestseller titled, *The Awesome Driven Life.*

4. The 360 review is a human resources tool that includes input from work peers or teammates in addition to the supervisor or manager. Rather than focusing on achievement, 360 review questions are designed to provide feedback that can be used to develop professional and interpersonal skills.

5. I believe this would be a good place to underscore how I view this search as a spiritual one that may or may not be supported by what are commonly defined as "traditional" spiritual practices. What becomes possible if we shift our focus from doing spiritual practices to being spiritual? I wrote a book about that! Meredith Gould, *Desperately Seeking Spirituality: A Field Guide to Practice* (Collegeville, MN: Liturgical Press, 2016).

6. Too rushed or busy to do the online search? For MBTI® visit The Myers & Briggs Foundation: www.myersbriggs.org. For The Enneagram visit The Enneagram Institute, which features the Riso-Hudson Enneagram Type Indicator (RHETI): www.enneagraminstitute.com. For the Strong® Career Test Online: http://bit.ly/2h1qHnZ. For MAPP™ Career Test: www.assessment.com.

7. Just a few examples: Catherine of Siena Institute, www.siena.org; "Exploring Your Spiritual Gifts," The United Methodist Church, http://bit.ly/2hq1S29; "Finding Your Spiritual Gifts," The Evangelical Lutheran Church in America, http://bit.ly/2hpY7d8 [pdf]; "Spiritual Gifts Test," giftstest.com (in partnership with beliefnet®): http://bit.ly/2hpXWhP.

8. In case you don't already have this earworm upon reading this verse, here you go—and you're welcome: https://youtu.be/W4ga_M5Zdn4.

Chapter 7: Belonging

1. Would this be a good time to mention that Dorothy Day titled her autobiography *The Long Loneliness* (New York: Harper & Row, 1952)? For what it's worth, Day's autobiography and the collection of Simone Weil's writings in *Waiting for God* (New York: G.P. Putnam, 1951) have helped me wrestle with issues of belonging to Christian community.

2. For details about how they distinguish the belongingness hypothesis from attachment theory à la John Bowlby, plow through Roy F. Baumeister and Mark R. Leary, "The Need to Belong: Desire for Interpersonal Attachments as a Fundamental Human Motivation," *Psychological Bulletin* 117, no. 3 (1995): 497–529, http://bit.ly/2hp5SV5.

3. The following is adapted from ibid.

4. For detailed data, see Pew Research Center, "The Return of the Multi-Generational Family Household," March 18, 2010, http://pewrsr .ch/2drjPeZ. See also Richard Fry, "More Millennials Living with Family despite Improved Job Market," July 29, 2015, Pew Research Center, http://pewrsr.ch/2drkFbU. For information and resources, visit Generations United, www.gu.org.

5. Health benefits of social contacts are so widely acknowledged that it can be considered what sociologists call a domain assumption, but if you need convincing, read: Erin York Cornwell and Linda J. Waite, "Social Disconnectedness, Perceived Isolation, and Health among Older Adults," *Journal of Health and Social Behavior* 50, no. 1 (2009): 31–48, http://bit .ly/2ichU0e [pdf].

6. For a detailed discussion about the power of online communities, especially in the world of church, read chapter 6, "Virtual Community is Real Community," in Meredith Gould, *The Social Media Gospel: Sharing the Good News in New Ways*, 2nd ed. (Collegeville, MN: Liturgical Press, 2015), 30–35. Although there's less resistance to digital ministry these days, I'm still compelled to emphasize that intergenerational collaboration cannot happen without it. Seriously. Cannot. Happen. Without. It.

7. Don't let the date of this journal article throw you; it's still a stellar read about the psychology of communities: David W. McMillan and David M. Chavis, "Sense of Community: A Definition and Theory," *Journal of Community Psychology* 14 (1986): 6–23, http://bit.ly/2deRhW7 [pdf].

8. Isolation, which means less social contact, is not the same thing is desolation, notes Henri J. M. Nouwen and Walter J. Gaffney in their book, *Aging: the Fulfillment of Life* (New York: Image Doubleday, 1976), 36: "Desolation is the crippling experience of the shrinking circle of friends with a devastating awareness that the few years left to live will not allow you to widen the circle again. Desolation is the gnawing feeling of being left behind by those who have been close and dear to you during the many years of life."

9. Marty Haugen, "All Are Welcome" (Chicago: GIA, 1994), http:// bit.ly/2mBGVrG.

10. I, for one, consider booking an extra psychotherapy session whenever I see this invitation. Family, really? Any guarantees it'll be any less dysfunctional than my—or anyone's—family of origin? Right, didn't think so.

11. I belonged to Alpha Xi Delta (Delta Lambda) chapter. After you finish laughing about this, be impressed by the fact that our chapter was threatened with expulsion for pledging a black woman . . . in 1971. We

flipped a collective finger at the national office and made her a sister. I still remember our secret knock.

12. A key feature of Cognitive Behavioral Therapy (CBT), "automatic thoughts" are thoughts that reflexively occur in the presence of a stimulus or trigger. Getting these thoughts into conscious awareness (i.e., cognitive restructuring) has been proven effective for dealing with anxiety and depression. For cognitive restructuring worksheets, see "Cognitive Restructuring," *Psychology Tools*, http://bit.ly/2dRLCbY.

13. Note slight differences in nomenclature for the liturgical calendar used by Catholics (i.e., Advent, Christmas, Ordinary Time, Lent, Easter, Ordinary Time) and Protestants (i.e., Advent, Christmas, Epiphany, Lent, Easter, Season after Pentecost).

14. Meredith Gould, *The Catholic Home: Celebrations and Traditions for Holidays, Feast Days, and Every Day* (New York: Image, 2004). Note: be sure to get the updated paperback edition. A free discussion guide is available on SlideShare: http://slidesha.re/nj4Uy9.

15. Read Michelle Van Loon, *Moments & Days: How Our Holy Celebrations Shape Our Faith* (Colorado Springs, CO: NavPress, 2016) along with Meredith Gould, *Why Is There a Menorah On the Altar? Jewish Roots of Christian Worship* (New York: Seabury, 2009).

Chapter 8: Legacy

1. Templates and guidelines for writing a living will are easily found via a Google search.

2. Visit the National Hospice and Palliative Care Organization's website, CaringInfo: http://bit.ly/2e1S41g.

3. To learn about the Jewish and biblical roots of ethical wills, see Jack Riemer and Nathaniel Stampfer, *So That Your Values Live On: Ethical Wills and How to Prepare Them* (Woodstock, VT: Jewish Lights, 1991) and *Ethical Wills: A Modern Jewish Treasury* (New York: Schocken, 1983). For an admirably comprehensive introduction to ethical wills (with links to examples, worksheets/templates, FAQs, and more), visit Pat McNees, "Have You Created a Legacy Letter or Ethical Will? Have You Received One?," http://bit.ly/2dRRJOy and The Legacy Project, www.you177.org.

4. Snapchat, a platform embraced almost exclusively by digital natives and originally promoted for the ephemeral quality of its content, now allows content to be collected as "memories" and saved. See Ash Read,

"Why Snapchat Memories Will Be Pivotal (And Why Marketers Are So Excited)," *Buffer Social*, July 27, 2016, http://bit.ly/2mBzCAm.

5. Over a decade ago, researchers at Microsoft reported that typical Internet users had at least twenty-five active online accounts. See Dinei Florencio and Cormac Herley, "A Large Scale Study of Web Password Habits," Microsoft Tech Report MSR-TR-2-6-166, November 1, 2006, http://bit.ly/2ep4iNr.

6. The go-to book is by Evan Carroll and John Romano, *Your Digital Afterlife: When Facebook, Flickr and Twitter Are Your Estate, What's Your Legacy?* (Berkeley, CA: New Riders, 2010), and visit their website, *The Digital Beyond*, which includes this "Digital Death and Afterlife Online Services List," http://bit.ly/2ep3gRG. See also Selina Ellis Gray and Paul Coulton, "Living with the Dead: Emergent Post-Mortem Digital Curation and Creation Practices," draft paper posted to academia.edu: http://bit.ly/2dTwFY5; and Jim Lamm, "Revised Uniform Fiduciary Access to Digital Assets Act," *Digital Passing: Estate Planning for Passwords and Digital Property* (blog), September 29, 2015: http://bit.ly/2dTxsbv.

7. To learn about the functionality available to a legacy contact, visit Facebook security settings and, while you're there, either designate someone or remember to do that sooner rather than later. Upon request, Facebook will also provide a "Looking Back" video of key moments and images generated from the deceased person's Facebook history.

8. Not my family! Conversations about dying, death, funeral arrangements, and the distribution of stuff was near constant. So was near-constantly adding and removing people from the last will and testament and discussing ways to get around trust and estate law. I have stories! Lots of stories about this family blood sport.

9. The Corporal Works of Mercy come to my mind, how about yours? I believe this might be the third book in which I (happily) provide this reminder to feed the hungry, shelter the homeless, clothe the naked, visit the sick and imprisoned, bury the dead, and give alms to the poor. More about this in chapter 8, "Generosity," in Meredith Gould, *Desperately Seeking Spirituality: A Field Guide to Practice* (Collegeville, MN: Liturgical Press, 2016), 58–67.

10. Chai there—again!

11. Wonder what's written on a mezuzah (Hebrew: doorpost) scroll? Wonder no longer! The scroll includes two verses (in Hebrew) from Deuteronomy (6:4-9; 11:13-21). What's a mezuzah scroll? It's the parchment

found in a mezuzah case affixed to the right side (as you enter) doorways in (some) Jewish homes. Note: entrances to rooms in addition to front and rear doorways.

Chapter 9: Listening

1. These days you can easily find resources for church communications in general and digital ministry in particular. Answered prayer—yours and mine—I am not stuffing this chapter with (much) of what I've already written in *The Social Media Gospel: Sharing the Good News in New Ways*, 2nd ed. (Collegeville, MN: Liturgical Press, 2015). I will, however, reiterate the value of observing, if not participating, in the Twitter-based weekly Church Social Media chat (#chsocm) and the (closed) Facebook group, Church Communications, http://bit.ly/2agMPsV. Through the power and glory of Google or search function of Facebook, you'll be able to find denomination-specific groups and organizations of church communicators.

2. Keeping in mind that human gestation is typically forty weeks, a fetus will begin hearing sound at eighteen weeks, become more sensitive to it at twenty-four weeks, and will respond to noise or voices at twenty-five to twenty-six weeks. Sound will be muffled because the uterus is a sealed environment, but there's plenty of research to indicate voice recognition—but that's not the same thing as listening. Also, there's no empirical evidence that playing classical music will enhance IQ or that saying nice things will enhance your baby's EQ (emotional quotient).

3. Alfred A. Tomatis, *The Conscious Ear: My Life of Transformation through Listening* (Barrytown, NY: Station Hill, 1992); *The Ear and the Language* (Toronto: Stoddart, 1997); *The Ear and the Voice* (Lanham, MD: Scarecrow, 2004). For analyses of the Tomatis Method, read Jan Gerritsen, "A Review of Research Done on Tomatis Auditory Stimulation," 2009: http://bit.ly/2mBSy1T; Tim Gilmor, "The Efficacy of the Tomatis Method for Children with Learning and Communication Disorders: A Meta-Analysis," *International Journal of Listening* 13, no. 1 (1999): 12–23, http://bit.ly/2am0Hz4.

4. Learning styles are yet another thing I'll probably be writing about forever. For my chart about relating learning styles to digital media platforms, see Meredith Gould, *The Social Media Gospel: Sharing the Good News in New Ways*, 2nd ed. (Collegeville, MN: Liturgical Press, 2015), 22. For my chart about learning styles relative to traditional spiritual practices, see

Desperately Seeking Spirituality: A Field Guide to Practice (Collegeville, MN: Liturgical Press, 2016), 14.

5. Marcia Reynolds, "How You Connect and Disconnect with Others: The 4 Dominant Communication Styles," *Outsmart Your Brain* (blog), http://bit.ly/2hHLCKm.

6. In this instance, I'm using the word "ecological" in the social-scientific sense of physical environment rather than as a reference to stewardship of God's creation—flora and fauna, etc.

7. Easily offended by so-called naughty words or swearing? Read Rebecca Roache, "Naughty Words" *Aeon*, February 22, 2016, http://bit .ly/2hrkkMs. For the origins of my fondness for swearing, read Meredith Gould, "About My 'Potty Mouth'," *Medium*, May 22, 2016, http://bit .ly/2hrebzH. As for irreverence, see Cindy Brandt, "Irreverence Is the New Reverent," *The Huffington Post*, July 22, 2014, http://huff.to/1nfCmMM. During Advent 2016, two ELCA pastors created *F*** This S****, a devotional quite unlike any other that because of its visceral language ended up attracting people who had given up on church and/or rarely participated in Advent devotions. I know this from doing my own text analysis of posted comments and tweets, and then spending some percentage of Advent inviting people to calm down long enough to notice its ministerial value. Before rushing to appalled judgment, please read Emily McFarlan Miller, "This Advent Devotional Uses Language You Won't Find in Scriptures," Religion News Service (RNS), December 1, 2016, http://bit.ly/2jG4z51; Alan Rudnick, "Advent Outrage: Would Jesus Curse?," *Alan Rudnick* (blog), December 1, 2016, http://bit.ly/2iIO8AJ.

8. Let me help you seem like a brainiac the next time you play Trivial Pursuit (if that's still a thing) by providing this detailed information about linguistics. Linguistics, the study of human language, includes these six subfields: (1) phonetics, studying physical aspects of speech sounds; (2) phonology, studying cognitive aspects of speech sounds; (3) morphology, studying word formation; (4) syntax, studying sentence formation; (5) semantics, studying meaning; and (6) pragmatics, studying language use.

9. Discover your stress level according to the Holmes-Rahe Life Stress Inventory (a.k.a. Social Readjustment Rating Scale, SRRS) at *Health Central*, http://bit.ly/2hrwdlB (provides online score calculation), or read the original by Thomas H. Holmes and Richard H. Rahe, "The Social Readjustment Rating Scale," *Journal of Psychosomatic Research* 11, no. 2 (1967): 213–18. See also the Perceived Stress Scale (PSS) at *Be Mindful*, http://

bit.ly/2hHO4R2, or read the original by Sheldon Cohen, Tom Kamarck, and Robin Mermelstein, "A Global Measure of Perceived Stress," *Journal of Health and Social Behavior* 24, no. 4 (1983): 385–96.

10. Ten speech elements women tend to use more frequently than men: hedging, politeness, tag questions, emotional emphasis, empty adjectives, correct grammar and pronunciation, lack of humor, direct quotations, extended vocabulary, and declarations with interrogative intonation. See Robin Lakoff, *Language and Woman's Place* (New York: Harper & Row, 1975).

11. Six main differences between female and male language use: status versus support; interdependence versus intimacy; advice versus understanding; information versus feelings; orders versus proposals; conflict versus compromise. See Deborah Tannen, *You Just Don't Understand: Men and Women in Conversation* (New York: Ballantine, 1990).

12. Leslie Kaufman, "For the Word on the Street, Courts Call Up an Online Witness," *New York Times*, May 20, 2013, http://nyti.ms/2asmQPs. For historical overview of *Urban Dictionary*, see this *Wikipedia* entry—and don't judge me for referencing *Wikipedia*: http://bit.ly/2asnhZX. If you're not easily offended, then enjoy Heather Barnett, "100 words from Urban Dictionary that Changed the World," *SheKnows*, May 25, 2016, http://bit.ly/2asnMmF.

Chapter 10: Decision-Making

1. Is "genuine collaboration" among clergy, religious, and laity possible in the Roman Catholic Church? I like this take on it by Fr. Michael Sweeney, OP, "Lay Collaboration in the Mission of the Church," Dominican School of Philosophy & Theology, http://bit.ly/2hv6DMr.

2. Just to be clear, I am not referring to members of the Religious Society of Friends (a.k.a. Quakers) for whom the Sense of the Meeting decision-making process requires patiently waiting for the Transition to Light, sometimes over a number of years. The Quaker approach is indeed an intentional activity of seeking divine wisdom through prayerful attention, as opposed to what shows up in too many other churches: passive aggression cleverly cloaked in *Robert's Rules of Order*. See Barry Morley, *Beyond Consensus: Salvaging Sense of the Meeting*, Pendle Hill Pamphlet 307 (Wallingford, PA: Pendle Hill, 1993).

3. Study this footnote and that person can be you! Consensual validation is the proposition that people have an inherent need to know (or believe) that other people feel, see, and understand things the way they

do. Early and most cited theory and research about this is from—1959. See Carl W. Backman and Paul F. Secord, "The Effect of Perceived Liking on Interpersonal Attraction," *Human Relations* 12, no. 4 (1959), 379–84, http://bit.ly/2hOfBjN.

4. Do you feel a sense of community in your home church (or any other organization)? Check it out by taking the Sense of Community Index 2 (SCI-2):© Background, Instrument, and Scoring Instructions (Gaithersburg, MD: Community Science, no year), http://bit.ly/2hOhWLN [pdf].

5. The "teachable moment" concept was popularized by physicist and education theorist Robert James Havighurst (1900–1991) in *Human Development and Education* (New York: D. McKay, 1953), 7. Physician and educator Maria Montessori (1870–1952) is also credited for highlighting teachable moments in her teaching philosophy and methodology.

6. Start with this article by Dave Roos, "How Generation Gaps Work," HowStuffWorks: Culture, http://bit.ly/2ifrlfK. Keep clicking through to find more information and resources about specific cohorts. See also Greg Hammill, "Mixing and Managing Four Generations of Employees," *FDU Magazine Online*, Winter/Spring 2005, http://bit.ly/2ifBWHj. For the motherlode of research go to the "Generations and Age" topic area at Pew Research Center, http://pewrsr.ch/2jeL2Z4.

7. Side Rant: I wish everyone would stop using "narcissism" to label what might be simple albeit annoying self-absorption. For the clinical definition of a Narcissistic Personality Disorder, see the American Psychiatric Association's DSM-IV and DSM-5 Criteria for Personality Disorders, http://bit.ly/2jwar0H.

8. Jerold Bozarth and Paul Wilkins, eds., *Unconditional Positive Regard*, Rogers Therapeutic Conditions Evolutionary Theory & Practice 3 (Ross-on-Wye, Herefordshire: PCCS, 2001).

9. Ah, feedback. The word has become code for "I'm going to slash you and your work into tattered ribbons of ego." Even I reflexively flinch when someone offers me feedback, which is amazing because I went to art school where the tradition of the weekly crit(ique) purified any egocentric sensitivities—by slashing me and my work into tattered ribbons of ego.

10. Demands by students for educators to provide advance warning about images, readings, and language that might trigger a PTSD response has generated some interesting (read: inflammatory) responses. The first epistle to spark a national conflagration was written by Dr. Everett Piper, president of Oklahoma Wesleyan University. On November 23, 2015,

he wrote a blog post titled, "This Is Not a Day Care. It's a University!," http://bit.ly/2hx8Ve8. In 2016, the Office of the Dean of Students at the College at the University of Chicago sent a letter to incoming students asserting that "we expect members of our community to be engaged in rigorous debate, discussion, and even disagreement. At times this may challenge you and even cause discomfort. Our commitment to academic freedom means that we do not support so-called 'trigger warnings'." Read the entire letter at http://bit.ly/2hOsmLx. For one response read what the Rev. Emily C. Heath has to say in "Trauma, Trigger Warnings, and Making a Little Space," Emily C. Heath (blog), August 27, 2016, http://bit.ly/2hOrLcN.

11. The expression "speak truth to power" is usually attributed to use by Quakers as early as the eighteenth century, although it entered contemporary usage when the American Friends Service committee published *Speak Truth to Power: A Quaker Search for an Alternative to Violence* in 1955. Civil rights activist Bayard Rustin is also credited for using the phrase in a letter he wrote in 1942. See John Green, "The Origin of the Phrase 'Speaking Truth to Power,'" Synonym.com: Classroom, http://bit.ly/2hVkSX1.

12. Roger Fisher and William Ury, *Getting to Yes: Negotiating Agreement without Giving In* (Boston: Houghton Mifflin, 1981); John Paul Lederach, *The Little Book of Conflict Transformation* (Intercourse, PA: Good Books, 2003). See especially the chart "Conflict Resolution and Conflict Transformation: A Brief Comparison of Perspective" on p. 33. Lederach is a sociologist who helped found the Conflict Transformation Program at Eastern Mennonite University during the 1990s.

13. The following is adapted from Roger Fisher and William Ury, *Getting to Yes: Negotiating Agreement without Giving In* (Boston: Houghton Mifflin, 1981).

Chapter 11: Embracing Change

1. Check out the choral arrangement and performance from a choir at St. Olaf College, "Saint Teresa's Bookmark," YouTube video, 3:56, from *A Thousand Ages: A Celebration of Hope* by St. Olaf Cantorei, dir. John Ferguson, provided to YouTube by CDBaby, posted by "St. Olaf Cantorei - Topic," August 28, 2015, http://bit.ly/2jkTbet. Also listen to the Taizé chant in Spanish: "Taizé - Nada te turbe," YouTube video, 4:50, music by J. Berthier, text by St. Teresa de Ávila, posted by "Mostar Taize," June 7, 2009, http://bit.ly/2ilmIRl.

2. I've made this newcomer mistake. Being on the receiving end of church leadership response was, shall we say, unpleasant.

3. Within recent history, the Second Vatican Council of the Roman Catholic Church (1962–65) and decades of subsequent changes provide an example of one way church-wide change happens. Another, more recent, one is the "Roman Missal Crisis" that started during the late 1990s and climaxed at the beginning of the liturgical year in 2011. For a timeline of changes from 1963 through 2010, see Rita Ferrone, "Roman Missal Crisis: A Timeline," *Commonweal,* June 30, 2011, http://bit.ly/2ixqZRF.

4. See the first stanza of Pierre Teilhard de Chardin, "Patient Trust," in *Hearts on Fire: Praying with Jesuits*, ed. Michael Harter, 102–3:

> Above all, trust in the slow work of God.
> We are quite naturally impatient in everything
>   to reach the end without delay.
> We should like to skip the intermediate stages. We are impatient of
>   being on the way to something
>   unknown, something new.
> And yet it is the law of all progress
>   that is made by passing through
>   some stages of instability—
>   and that may take a very long time.

The entire poem appears in Matt Emerson, "The Slow Work of God," The Ignatian Educator, *America*, December 11, 2014, http://bit.ly/2mbcaXq.

5. Physicist and social scientist Kurt Lewin called this period of uncertainty and confusion the "Unfreeze" stage of this three-stage change management model. The second stage, "Change," is identifiable because everyone pretty much calms down and starts supporting new ways of being and doing in an organization. Organizations will "Refreeze" when the changes become business-as-usual. Kurt Lewin, "Frontiers in Group Dynamics: Concept, Method and Reality in Social Science; Social Equilibria and Social Change," *Human Relations* 1 (1947): 5–41, http://bit.ly/2jB9qUS [pdf].

6. The following is adapted from William Bridges, *Transitions: Making Sense of Life's Changes,* rev. ed. (Cambridge, MA: Da Capo, 2004) and *Managing Transitions: Making the Most of Change*, 3rd ed. (Cambridge, MA: Da Capo, 2009).

7. Quoting myself: "Dig into the anger and discover disappointment; dig deeper through the disappointment and discover grief. Dig into the indignation and discover vulnerability; dig deeper through the vulnerability

and discover fear." See Meredith Gould, *Desperately Seeking Spirituality: A Field Guide to Practice* (Collegeville, MN: Liturgical Press, 2016), 51.

8. "We have always had ____" and "We don't do it that way" are two of the five phrases Rev. Alan Rudnick identifies as especially frustrating to Millennials. I agree wholeheartedly but wish to note that four phrases on his list irk the snot out of Boomers as well. Which ones? Read and decide: Alan Rudnick, "5 Phrases that Frustrate Millennials in Church," *Alan Rudnick* (blog), April 14, 2015, http://bit.ly/2i8d844.

9. John Tierney, "What Is Nostalgia Good For? Quite a Bit, Research Shows," *New York Times*, July 7, 2013, http://nyti.ms/2iDdOyD. For a brief history of nostalgia, see Neel Burton, "The Meaning of Nostalgia," *Psychology Today*, November 27, 2014, http://bit.ly/2jBhbKB. For published research from the Nostalgia Group at the University of Southampton, see http://bit.ly/2ixumbr, as well as the Southampton Nostalgia Scale: http://bit.ly/2jwoDXg [pdf].

10. Congregational change management is usually called "congregational development" and/or a variation on mission "development" or "mission redevelopment." In addition to being seminary educated, experts in church change management are usually well-versed in work of the secular experts in change management mentioned in this chapter, as well as thought leaders who have developed the theory and practice of "learning organizations" (e.g., Chris Argyris, Peter Senge, Margaret J. Wheatley).

11. The following is adapted from John P. Kotter and Leonard A. Schlesinger, "Choosing Strategies for Change," *Harvard Business Review*, July–August 2008 (reprint of original article from 1979), http://bit.ly/2j0E4GZ.

Appendix: A Listening 101

1. When I was growing up, saying "shut up" was considered a serious verbal offense that guaranteed a sojourn in my bedroom to "think about it." Today, whether "shut up" is considered a rude way to silence someone depends on delivery. Notice what happens when a pause is added between "shut" and "up" and then "up" is uttered with lilting exuberance: shut—*up*! Now it's an expression of astonishment with an inherent invitation to reveal more: "[Shut *up*!] Wow, seriously? Tell me! Really, don't leave anything out."

2. Not to brag (much) but my eye-rolling is so advanced that I don't even have to use emojis or GIFS for people to know when I'm doing it

while posting to social media. As for childhood threats by my mother, my face has yet to "freeze that way." I think.

3. Why bother providing nonverbal listening cues when part of a large audience? I invite you to recall what you've seen from the podium/lectern/pulpit/ambo. In addition to seeing predictable stuff like smiling, frowning, and fidgeting, I've seen people adjust underwear, explore their nose for boogers, and more! And not just during keynotes, lectures, and workshops but also during worship.

4. I confess to almighty God (who already knows this about me) and to you, my sisters and brothers, that I have yet to master this "don't interrupt" thing. I've been known to interrupt myself. In my own defense, I believe part of this is regional and ethnic.

Appendix B: Decision-Making 101

1. I'm a big fan of Appreciative Inquiry (AI), which helps participants focus their attention on what is working well, what has worked well, and how to keeping doing what works well. See "The Best of AI Web Sites," *Appreciative Inquiry Commons*, http://bit.ly/2h034NO. See also the Center for Appreciative Inquiry, www.centerforappreciativeinquiry.net. Probably not-so-strange and true: I was a fan of parliamentary procedure during young adulthood and had my very own copy of *Robert's Rules of Order*. See Henry M. Robert III and Daniel H. Honemann, *Robert's Rules of Order Newly Revised*, 11th ed. (Cambridge, MA: Da Capo, 2011); C. Alan Jennings, *Robert's Rules for Dummies*, 3rd ed. (Hoboken, NJ: John Wiley, 2016).

2. "Sense of the Meeting" refers specifically to a process embraced by the Religious Society of Friends (Quakers). As explained by Barry Morley, it is "never consensus" and comes from a "commitment to continuing revelation." Morley has also observed that "the sense of the meeting is a Quaker equivalent of Communion." Barry Morley, *Beyond Consensus: Salvaging Sense of the Meeting*, Pendle Hill Pamphlet 307 (Wallingford, PA: Pendle Hill, 1993). For more about how Quakers deal with sincere expressions of difference, read: Eden Grace, "An Introduction to Quaker Business Practice" (paper presented at a subcommittee meeting of the Special Commission on Orthodox Participation in the World Council of Churches, Damascus, Syria, March 2000), http://bit.ly/2gNadNR.

3. While consensus currently seems to be the preferred decision rule in church communities, it can be confused with agreement. Consensus is,

more accurately, unanimous consent. Dissenters are willing to "live with" decisions for the sake of unity—real or imagined.

4. Celebrate unanimity with extreme caution because what looks like unanimous agreement might be for one issue only and not represent group alignment on *anything* else. Think about how many times you've allowed a group decision with which you did not agree to move forward because you could not stand another nanosecond of—anything. Even worse, unanimity might be covering up shadow side stuff like intimidation.

Subject Index

Scripture Index